The Book of Tap

THE BOOK OF TAP

Recovering America's Long Lost Dance

Jerry Ames
and
Jim Siegelman

David McKay Company, Inc.   New York

To Mom, who was a mother at every stage, but never a stage mother.

Jerry Ames

To Kurt.

Jim Siegelman

Library of Congress Cataloging in Publication Data

Ames, Jerry.
  The book of tap.

  1. Tap dancing. I. Siegelman, Jim, joint
author. II. Title.
GV1794.A45   793.3'24   76-44412
ISBN 0-679-50615-2
ISBN 0-679-50632-2 pbk.

10 9 8 7 6 5 4 3 2 1

MANUFACTURED IN THE UNITED STATES OF AMERICA

Acknowledgments

Except for four people, everyone who helped with *The Book of Tap* appears in it somewhere. We are extremely grateful to David Currier, general editor of the project, without whose direction, patience, skill, and care the book would not have come about. I would also like to express personal thanks to Flo Conway, whose poetry, theory, and editorial expertise were of inestimable value in the book's design and development. And my thanks to Donald Farber, who served as catalyst in bringing together everyone involved. And lastly Scott Star, for his patience and talent and for his wonderful photographs.

Jerry Ames

Jim Siegelman

Contents

Introduction

by
Eleanor Powell

Tap is our American folk dance. It is the red, white, and blue. I don't know how else to explain it. Imagine how Hawaii would feel if the hula went out of fashion. You expect a lei to be put around your neck and to see the dancers—that's part of the tradition. In the same way, tap, on the mainland, is our indigenous national rhythmic dance. It is the uniquely American contribution to the world of dance.

Ironically, as a child I loathed tap dancing because I was very involved in ballet, which I adored—"very square," you might say. Incidentally, I believe ballet is the foundation of all dancing! I started dancing professionally in Atlantic City when I was thirteen years old. I danced before an audience three times a week, and I got seven dollars a night—twenty-one dollars a week. When I was fifteen, I became the Mistress of Ceremonies at the Silver Slipper in Atlantic City and had to introduce the various acts. Among them would always be a few "hoofers," and with disdain I looked upon them. "Ugh!" I said. "I don't like that at all."

Then came the irony. When I went to New York, the first agent's opening question was "Do you tap?" No. Then "Do you tap?" from the next agent. No. Finally, in desperation, I asked one of them, "Where can I learn how to tap dance? Where do you suggest?" He said, "Why don't you go to the Jack Donahue School of Dance?" (Jack Donahue was Marilyn Miller's dancing partner from England.) So I went there, and because a series of ten lessons was cheaper than an individual lesson, I took the series and paid thirty-five dollars. That's what it cost me to learn to tap dance.

At the first lesson, they took me into a room—I've never seen this done since—and asked me to beat out a rhythm on the table, I guess to see if I had any natural sense of rhythm in me. Then I went into the beginners' classroom, in the back row. They started to teach a time step—I had no idea what it was at that time—and the pupils seemed to pick up the first step fairly easily. Then they went on to the second step, and I didn't even have the first step down, and then they hit us with the first step added to the second step, and I didn't know either step. It went on like that, and when the class was over, my mother, who was waiting for me in the dressing room, said, "How did it go?" And I said, "No way. I despise it. I can't . . ." Mother said, "Forget it." I said, "What about the thirty-five dollars we've paid?" And she said, "Well, if you don't like it and you can't get it, just forget it." So the next lesson I didn't attend.

When the following lesson day came around, the phone rang. It was Mr. Donahue, who said, "Aren't you the little girl who wasn't in class last Tuesday?" I said, "Mr. Donahue, I'm sorry. It isn't your fault; it's mine. But first of all, I don't care for it. I just don't seem to be able . . . I don't understand it. And I just can't do it." He said, "Well, now, wait a minute. Wait a minute. Suppose you come back to the next class, and I will watch you individually and see if I can sort of help you with what troubles you." I was angry with myself and so I said, "All right. I'll go back and try again." Well, the second was no better than the first. I remember it vividly. He was sitting on the windowsill wearing a felt hat, pulled down, while his assistant taught the class. I was in the back row, and he was watching me, and when the class was over, I had done no better.

At that time they had small, private cubicles where for a dollar you could rehearse what you had just learned, to practice and get it in your memory. Mr. Donahue took me into the little private room and said, "Now, what seems to be the trouble?" I explained it to him. Then he said, "Well, first of all, you're very turned out, and tap dancing, you know, makes all the different muscles *exactly* the opposite from ballet, *exactly opposite*." He went on, "You're also very aerial; in tap, you've got to get down to the floor. I think I've got an idea. Anyway, we'll try it." So that time we did no steps; he just talked to me. "You come back next Tuesday."

I went back into the class, in the back row—and did a tiny bit better. Then we went into the private room again. This time he had a war surplus belt, the kind that you put bullets in. There weren't any bullets, but on each side of the belt were two sandbags—the kind they use to weigh down the curtains in the theater. I want you to know that with that belt on I couldn't move off the floor, and I haven't moved off the floor since. That's why I dance so close to the ground, because Donahue started me with fundamentals, just as one would do scales on the piano.

Tap dancing often requires a "shifting of gears," as in an automobile engine. When he had me wear those sandbags, I thought, "This is really stupid." He had me stand there and shift my weight from the right hip to the left and back. I must have done it for half an hour, all the time thinking, "This is tap?" for I wasn't making any sound. But this is one of the most important things you can learn in tap dancing, because when you end a step and your weight is on, say, your right foot, although the left foot is free you sometimes have to start the next step with the foot your weight is on—in this case, the right foot. So this shifting of gears is essential to know.

After I started with the sandbags, the next lesson was a little better. Then it was back into the private room for more work with the sandbags, and somehow—I just can't explain it—in about the seventh lesson it all came together. Just like an algebra problem—you have a tutor teaching you and all of a sudden you say, "Oh, now I see!" At the end of the tenth lesson I was up with Mr. Donahue demonstrating the routine that previously I hadn't gotten at all. And later, when I auditioned, the only thing I knew in tap was that routine, which I did in my first show. I didn't know anything else.

From then on, I started making up my own steps. On matinee days, when everybody would go out to eat, I would have a malted milk or a sandwich in the dressing room. The theater would be dark, with just the work lights on, and I'd go down and put a Fats Waller record on the Victrola—at that time you had to crank it—and rehearse and rehearse, by myself, trying to perfect this, trying to perfect that. Mr. Donahue had said, "You can combine your ballet with your tap." What he meant was "taps on turns," syncopated taps while you are pirouetting. And I worked. It took me three years to accomplish syncopated taps while turning. And I would rehearse right up to half-hour. The ushers would be coming down the aisles with their programs and so forth, getting the seats ready. Then half-hour would be called, and I'd go up and take a quick shower, slop on the makeup, and that night give a very . . . well, let's say, not as good a performance as I could have, because I was exhausted, but at the same time *delighted* that—to me, for myself—I had accomplished something in that dark theater.

I lived and breathed dance. I never knew there was an outside world. My mother used to kid me and say, "I never had a daughter; I always had a star." What she meant was a daughter who knew how to iron and shop. I was always in a rehearsal hall.

I used to dream my best ideas. In my dream I would *see* it, and I'd wake up . . . I kept a pencil by the night stand and I'd jot the idea down in shorthand—hoofer shorthand—and the next day I'd work out the dance. I would actually *see* combinations of steps. And everything I looked at was a source. I'd see a sunset and get an idea for a number. It got so that everything was dance.

Fred Astaire also received inspiration from his dreams. When we were rehearsing for *Broadway Melody of 1940* I mentioned my dreaming and he said, "This is what *I* do! I *dream* this stuff, and I get up and write." In the beginning, however, we were not so familiar. He told me that as I was the first woman he ever worked with who did her own choreography, he wasn't about to tell *me* what to do, and of course, *I* wasn't about to tell Mr. Astaire what to do. We had five numbers altogether in Melody of Forty, and of course the producers and everybody else thought that this would be like two champion boxers getting together—it was supposed to fracture the whole world. A great deal was expected of us. Cole Porter had written "Begin the Beguine," and I had had my pianist play it over beforehand, and I had some ideas in mind; and Mr. Astaire, who was in London visiting his sister, also had it played—he probably played it himself because he plays beautifully—and he had some ideas of *his* own.

The day we first met I said, "What time would you like to rehearse, Mr. Astaire?" He said, "Oh, whatever time Miss Powell would like." I said, "Oh, no, whatever time *you* would like." This went on for a while, and finally I said, "Well, how about eight o'clock? Is that too early?" "No, that's perfect." So we met at eight at the east gate and were sauntering nonchalantly down the studio lot, making this very lovely prittle-prattle about his trip, and all the while I was dying to get to the fundamentals. Finally we came to the bungalow that Mr. Mayer had built for me—a lovely rehearsal hall with two dressing rooms and two baths—and I said to Mr. Astaire, "Your dressing room is in there. I'll change and meet you in a few minutes." "Thank you very much." Very polite.

I had told Mr. Astaire previously that he could bring his own piano player. I had said, "I know how important it is for you to have your own man. You're a guest on the lot; it's all new to you; and I want you to be as comfortable as you possibly can." "Well, that's very kind of you," he said. When we found out that RKO musicians could not come over to Metro, we used Walter, my man, who was very good. But naturally I wanted him to feel at home, and I did everything but play the Japanese Geisha. So we sat there, in two directors' chairs, and he said, "Would you like to hear the music?" I said, "Yes. That would be fine. Walter, would you mind?" Walter played "Begin the Beguine." By this time, of course, we knew it backwards. When it was finished, Mr. Astaire said, "Would you like to hear it again?" I thought, *Uhhh!* I said, "Fine." Walter played it again and I thought, We're contracted, we're signed, and we have to *begin*. We had five numbers, and from that moment on, the clock was ticking off the time. What are we going to do?, I thought. Finally I said, "Mr. Astaire, I have a number. There's something wrong in the middle of it somewhere. If I do it for you, would you be kind enough to help me with it? To tell me what you think?" He said, "Oh, I'd be delighted." So I got up and danced, and eventually I said, "You see . . . right here. . . ." And he got off his chair and said, "Yes, I see what you mean. Well, now, maybe, I think if . . ." And he did something. And then he realized he was on his feet. He looked at me and said, "Oh . . . Oh . . ." and rushed back and sat down. You have never seen such mutual respect. It was like two interior decorators: One wants blue and the other one wants pink, so you have to make it pinkish-blue.

So I said, "Mr. Astaire, you know, I don't know what we're going to do. I have some ideas, but I'm certainly not going to tell *you* anything." And he said the same to me. I said, "Well, if it meets with your approval, suppose I go over there in the corner, and Walter plays eight bars, and I just sort of noodle around, and you go over there and do the same thing, and if you see something you like, stop me, and vice versa, and maybe we can cut it, blend it . . ." And that's the way we started.

The first day nothing much happened because we were both sort of tight and strained. In fact, it was "Miss Powell" and "Mr. Astaire" for three or four days before the formality broke down. Then one day we did a step a little different but with the same rhythm, and he forgot himself and ran over and lifted me up in the air and said, "Oh, Ellie, that's . . ." He stopped himself and put me down, saying, "Oh, I do beg your pardon." Then I said,

INTRODUCTION

"Now listen. Fundamentally we are hoofers, right? We are the act that opens first with the flea circus. You may be the great Mr. Astaire and all that, but we are still hoofers, so can we get down to 'Ellie' and 'Fred'?" And then the ice broke, and he hugged me, and it was off to the races from then on.

A lot of tap numbers from films and shows have been re-released on records lately, which reminds me of how recording technology used to be. While I was in New York doing a Broadway show, RCA asked me to make two records with Tommy Dorsey's orchestra, which had been in a movie with me. One side of each record was to be from the show, and the flip side, one of the numbers from the movie. Everything was fine until we got over to RCA and discovered that they had completely forgotten all about the fact that I was going to sing *and* tap dance. There were thick, plush rugs everywhere, and they said, "Oh! Oh, my Lord, we for . . . Oh! . . ." There wasn't a piece of linoleum around or anything, and here was Tommy Dorsey's orchestra being paid some fabulous amount per hour. And the fellow in charge was tearing his hair out. I said, "Well, get a little portable tap mat." They called all the dancing schools and just couldn't find one. So I said, "Wait a minute. Let me think." I walked down to the floor below where they were going to record—and where there were offices, with doors. I said, "If you could take one of those doors off the hinges, I think I can manage there." And it worked fine, except that I wanted a vamp exit, the kind where it gets fainter and fainter and fainter, and they didn't have the equipment that would produce that effect. Today, with stereo and echo chambers and the like, you can do it easily, but at that time they couldn't. So we improvised, using a rope, and what you hear today on those old records is me tap dancing on a door and a prop man slowly pulling me with the rope further and further from the orchestra to make the sound fade in the distance.

There are many, many stories about the world of tap, and I've shared a few of mine with you. In *The Book of Tap,* Jerry Ames and Jim Siegelman seek to tell the story of tap dance from its earliest origins through the minstrel, vaudeville, Broadway, and Hollywood periods. It includes some fascinating comments by professionals and amateurs, as well as instructional material and other valuable information, along with a wealth of photographs. I hope you like it, as I love tap. More than anything in the world. Dance was always to me like some kind of idol, sitting up there saying, "You belong to me. I possess you. You work! You work!" There's no other outside—no dating, no boyfriends, no nothing. Just go to bed, get your rest, eat well, take your vitamins—and work.

Now I've just turned sixty-four, and I still tap dance every day. I'd rather dance than eat, or live, or whatever. That's it! Born to Dance.

Being a rhythm dancer has brought me a long way. I believe I have the feet of a percussion instrument and the soul of a violin. Who could ask for anything more?

—*Eleanor Powell*

Eleanor Powell—perhaps the greatest female tapper of films
(MGM Studio Shot).
New York Public Library.

The Book of Tap

Best Foot Foreword

One-two-three-four, one-two-three-and

STAMP! Hop shuffle–step,

Flap-left, step STAMP—reverse!

Hop shuffle–step,

Flap-right, step STAMP—break!

Hop shuffle–step, shuffle–step, shuffle–hop,

Flap-right, step STAMP!

A mother sparrow teaching her young to fly? A copy of the new post office motto? Not at all. You have just crossed over the boundary of your ordinary, everyday, flat-footed world and entered the exuberant, glamorous, quick-stepping, elegant realm of America's gift to dance—tap.

Shuffle, step–heel; shuffle, step–heel—the suave, masculine world of Fred Astaire and Gene Kelly. *Hop–shuffle, step–shuffle*—the confident feminine world of Eleanor Powell and Ann Miller. *Flap flap flap*—the happy sound of the great musical comedies, the syncopated beat of jazz, the magic and glitter of the Golden Age of Hollywood. *Shuffle–cramp roll, shuffle–cramp roll*—the steamer trunk and the concert stage: Ruby Keeler, Ray Bolger, Ginger Rogers, Donald O'Connor, Shirley Temple, Dan Dailey, Paul Draper . . .

Break–two–three–and—

Tap is the blend of cultures that makes up America—Barney Fagan and the Irish jig; Juba and the African stomp; Pat Rooney and the waltz clog. It's George M. and Mr. Bojangles and Jim Crow and Old Dan Tucker. The soft shoe, the Cakewalk, the Stair Dance, the Funky Butt. It's *Follies, Blackbirds, Scandals, Hoofers, Gold Diggers,* "Yankee Doodle Dandy," "The Good Ship Lollipop," and *Broad-way rhy-thm it's got me.*

Hop shuffle–hop, shuffle–ball change,

Hop shuffle–hop, shuffle–ball change,

Hop shuffle–hop, shuffle–ball change,

. . . Whew!

Tap dancing is back. It's not clear just why or how it got away in the first place, but it has been rediscovered in our time, and renewed. Tap has returned as entertainment, as recreation, as an evolving art form. It has gradually resurfaced to assume, once again, its rightful place in our popular culture, and now it's ready to move with us into the future.

The rebirth of tap in the 1970s is a curious thing. There had been virtually no tap dancing in American entertainment for nearly a generation. Then, several years ago, a few of the old stage and film musicals reappeared. First Ruby Keeler returned to Broadway in a revival of the 1920s musical *No, No, Nanette*. Then MGM released *That's Entertainment*—in two dazzling and successful installments—featuring the best scenes from the great tap dancing musicals of the thirties and forties. Coincidentally, dance classes around the country began to fill up with housewives, office workers, schoolteachers, businessmen, and all kinds of other people you would never expect to find lacing up a pair of tap shoes. At the same time, singers, dancers, actors, and other show people started thinking that maybe they ought to polish up those rusty old tap steps they learned back when they were apple-cheeked child stars in the dancing school recital.

Just like that, the appreciation of tap dancing was revived in America. A few more musicals were dusted off. Late-shows reeled through whole weeks of Fred Astaire festivals. Choreographers and theater critics began to take note, and all the while amateur hoofers kept legging it to their tap classes, puffing and wheezing to Hops and Leaps and Cramp Rolls, trying their damnedest to remember the most elementary tap routines, humming cheery numbers like "Once in Love with Amy" and "Tea for Two," while their baffled-but-pleased tap instructors created simple, rhythmic tap combinations designed to be executed by even the minimally talented.

Amidst all this glorious clacking some people have begun to reflect upon what tap dancing really is—the special mix of rhythm, sound, movement, and indefinable style that constitutes this American art form. Others have discovered that, more than anything else, tap is great fun—to do as well as to watch.

So it seemed like a good time to write a book of tap, one that would tell, in words and pictures, the surprising story of where tap dancing came from, one that would give the reader some understanding of what tap has been and is now, and how it differs from other forms of dance. Above all, we wanted to present real people—professionals and amateurs—talking about tap: how the form developed, what it's like, and what it can become.

So after hours of homework in libraries and museums, we set out with high hopes to find out what living tappers had to say. First we checked around the country to see what's going on in the nation's dancing schools and to discover people's reasons for taking up tap. Then we tried to get in touch with some of the great tap stars to hear what they think of this resurgence of interest in a dance form that supposedly died out in the fifties. We threw our nets wide yet again, casting for dance critics, choreog-

4

raphers, and rising young tap stars to get some ideas about where tap dancing is headed in the future. The result is a narrative in which many voices speak besides our own, providing what we hope is an intimately balanced view of the world of tap.

We decided to close our book on an ambitious note by trying to offer some instruction in tap dancing. Of course, you can't really learn to tap dance from a book, but what we've put in print can serve as a helpful supplement to the steps and routines you learn in tap class from a qualified tap instructor.

Virtuoso tap dancing is a serious activity that takes years of training, practice, and performance to master; but tap can also mean good exercise and great fun for the amateur enthusiast. So brush up your top hat, strap on your black patents . . . let's lay down some iron and shuffle off to Buffalo:

> Step-right, shuffle-left, step-left,
>
> Step-right, shuffle-left, step-left,
>
> Step-right, shuffle-left, step-left . . . (repeat to Buffalo)

Jerry Ames
Jim Siegelman

CHAPTER ONE

Tap Patter

Nobody's fallen down. Everybody's giggled a lot, but we all take it
quite seriously.

—**Rosemary Berry**
amateur tapper
New York, New York

I'm definitely an amateur. We're doing a recital on Sunday and I think we
look pretty silly. I've been in it a year and I really don't feel like I'm ready
for a recital.

—**Lisa Bradley**
amateur tapper
Los Angeles, California

A new breed of tap dancer has appeared in dance studios across the
country. Unlike traditional students of the dance, these tappers don't think
in terms of auditions or callbacks. They have a relaxed attitude toward
training and dedication, and they evaluate their performance according to
alien standards of *noise, stamina, therapy,* and *kicks.* They are amateur
tappers, and their numbers have grown ever larger in recent years. What
has drawn them to tap?

It keeps you young. I'm middle-aged and I wanted to do something besides
knit and crochet and play bridge. So I took tapping, and I'm doing quite
well. It's made me limber. A lot of women my age can't even bend down
and pick up a pencil. I struggle, though, I really struggle, but I wouldn't
let the young kids outdo me. So I just went home and practiced and pretty
soon I got it going.

—**Louise Woodward**
amateur tapper
Chicago, Illinois

In deciding to take up tap, some amateurs act on impulse; others give the decision months of painful deliberation. But they all have one thing in common: Once they start tapping, they love it. But just what is its appeal?

> We've got to think about the dancing, just watching what the teacher shows us and trying to get our brains to send the messages to our feet. It's different from what the average housewife does at home.
> —**Rosemary Kendrick**
> amateur tapper
> Chicago, Illinois

Tap dancing *is* different. It takes people out of their ordinary world, offering a new and different type of stimulation that is a welcome break from the chores and drudgery of everyday living. What's more, it can teach you things about yourself that you might not learn any other way.

> During the winter I am a ski instructor. My skiing got to sort of a plateau level, and I was impressed by the fact that some of the girls who had had tap dancing were a lot lighter on their feet and they could pick up skiing easier. So I thought, well, I'll try it myself. One thing I discovered is that I walk on the back of my heels, which is the problem with my skiing, that I'm always falling backwards. So it's already helped that, at least it gets the weight up forward on my toes.
> —**Rob Hess**
> amateur tapper
> San Francisco, California

Whatever people's reasons, it is apparent that unusual forces have been at work. At the moment of inception of this grass roots movement, homemakers, students, and executives began sneaking away from their houses, classrooms, and offices for about an hour each week. They would reappear without explanation, in those early days, looking very much the same as before, yet different somehow—a change had come over them. They seemed happier, definitely, but slightly guilty about something.

Little was said about it at first, as though it were a deep, dark secret. People seemed embarrassed, ashamed, afraid to admit that they were taking *tap dancing* lessons. They would hide their tap shoes in the back of the car. They would say they were going off to the laundry or to meet an old friend. Housewives would leave their children with a neighbor in the middle of the day. Businessmen would tell their colleagues they had to go home early and tell their wives they had to work late. In this manner, the tap revival started underground. Back then, everyone made some excuse for where he or she was going.

Eventually, as enthusiasts discovered each other and gained confidence in their abilities, tappers began to come out in the open.

> I've taken a lot of ribbing. I work for the city and county of San Francisco—I'm a payroll clerk—and I practice during my lunch hour. They have this large lunchroom and hardly anybody's in there. So I take my tape recorder and tape the music and do my exercises and tap dance in this huge room. I just move all the chairs and tables back. Sometimes, when there's nobody around but the co-workers, I'll fool around. Maybe I'll shuffle to the files. Why not?
>
> **—Lee Benita**
> amateur tapper
> San Francisco, California

Today there's a new boldness among amateur tappers. They're no longer afraid to tap out loud. Moreover, the contemporary attitude of "do your own thing" has freed many who were previously too inhibited. You don't have to flaunt your tap skills and be a show-off, but there's no reason to refrain from tapping just because you're not on stage. And besides, a person's got to get in some practice here and there.

> I usually practice while I'm fixing dinner in the kitchen. Shuffles, a little ball change, whatever I have learned that week, if I can remember it. I also tend to practice out in the hall of my apartment building where there's a marble floor and mirrors on both sides. I'm not quite sure how people react to it.
>
> **—Gretchen Troster**
> amateur tapper
> San Francisco, California

For more and more tappers, it doesn't matter how people react. People may make fun, they may appear to be shocked, but more often than not, they're just jealous. So unless you're in church, the library, or a burning skyscraper, don't worry about what people around you are saying.

9

I work at the Railroad Retirement Board. I practice under my desk or waiting for the elevator. If I get a difficult claim or something, my feet just automatically break out into dance. And in the washroom, when I'm waiting to wash my hands, I'll start shuffling. People say, "We'll be right with you," and I say, "Take your time. I'm just practicing." I formed the habit of practicing at the bus stop, too. In the wintertime, people say, "Maybe she's cold," and in the summertime they say, "Maybe the heat's got her." I don't break out into dance, but I will move my feet, and people will say, "Oh, she's dancing. She must feel good." And they come over and say, "Oh, a rainy day and you feel so good." And I say, "Oh, yes, I feel fine," and I just keep on going.

— **Louise Woodward**

It would be wrong, however, to conclude from the foregoing that tap dancing, or even taking tap lessons, is always easy.

It's really hard, it's not easy at all, and it's frustrating. I'm disappointed because I can't do it that well, but I'm going to keep with it. I hoped I would catch on easier than I have, but it's not any natural feeling for me. It just doesn't come naturally.

— **Lisa Bradley**

This frustration is a perfectly normal feeling, one that all amateur tappers must come to terms with. It's a state of mind you pass through eventually, and finally that glorious day comes when you feel it all click. Somewhere, in your head, in your feet, the whole thing comes together. The steps begin to turn out right, the body starts to throw itself naturally into each movement. Whole dance routines seem to remember themselves at will, and you can at last stop concentrating long enough to enjoy what you're doing.

Congratulations! You've become a tap dancer!

On the other hand, that weary, plodding feeling may fail to resolve itself. You may struggle for weeks and months, still convinced that you've made no progress whatsoever, or that there's not a beat of rhythm in your body. You may feel uncoordinated, stupid, hopeless, a totally unworthy example of a human being. With every step you take, you become more and more convinced that you're making a complete and utter fool of yourself.

Congratulations! Now you've learned the true meaning of the word *amateur!*

It's nothing to be ashamed of. The truth of the matter is that the amateurs helped immeasurably to bring back tap dancing. There were no massive advertising campaigns from the dance instructors' union, no hard-sell commercial assaults from the makers of metal taps or hardwood floors, and, contrary to widespread opinion, the press had very little to do with the tap revival. A few articles in national magazines reacted with amusement or bewilderment to the emerging tap phenomenon; several local television stations produced tap specials in response to audience requests. But to a great extent it is ordinary people who have brought back the interest in tap dancing—not the entertainment moguls, not the news media—and the story of tap's popular rebirth is an inspiring one.

All this activity has taken dance teachers by surprise. There have always been amateur dancers, but never before has a dance been mobilized to

serve such a wide variety of purposes. The dance teachers we spoke with for this book were former dancing stars, current professional dancers, and choreographers from Broadway to Hollywood. They all have standards they go by, special approaches to tap technique or instruction; and they all had to adjust their teaching careers in response to the hordes of amateurs enrolling in tap classes across the land. Depending on which section of the country we queried, enrollment in tap classes was said to be double, triple, quadruple, and in one case a hundred times what it had been a few years earlier. Teachers explained some of the adjustments they had to make.

> These people come in and usually they're very reluctant, even though they want to do it. They're afraid of tap because they've always seen it done professionally. We let them come in. We have what we call our Guest Lesson—they can come in for the first lesson and try it for free—and we show them by the end of the first lesson that they're actually dancing already. We don't just make them go through the steps. We actually begin to teach them to dance, and they go out of here feeling that they're already Fred Astaire or Ginger Rogers.
>
> —**Al Gilbert**
> tap instructor
> Los Angeles, California

Teachers know that it's easy to get discouraged at a first tap lesson. The great tappers all make it look so easy, and once a student finds out that he can't just tie his shoes and launch into a barrel roll, it's not unusual for him to feel as if he's wasting his time. As with any discipline, it takes great effort to learn to tap dance—and long, hard hours of work. But there's a simplicity to tap dancing; there's something very straightforward and uncomplicated about the art. It's part of what makes great tapping look so graceful and effortless, and an amateur can begin to understand this from the very first lesson.

> People come to dance lessons for various reasons. They don't all come to dance. They come for maybe a therapeutic situation or to lose weight. Maybe some of them have their head in the clouds and feel they're going to have a dance career. Teaching is not really teaching; it's a very involved kind of thing. I have people that walk out and I have people that flip their lids.
>
> —**Toni Ambrosio**
> tap instructor
> Los Angeles, California

All kinds of forces are at work in tap class. If nothing else, it gives the instructor an opportunity to learn something, too. Tap teachers used to concentrate on their feet. Now, however, they have to spend time thinking about entire people. It may create a whole new class of professional person: the dancing psychologist.

> See, a man's work is interesting to others, but to himself it's work. This gives them a chance to get out. I have quite a number of amateurs. A couple of them were so bad, it was brutal, but the desire led them to where they were proficient. I teach two doctors; I've got three grandmothers. In fact, I

12

just had a recital and my doctor who operated on me for prostate was in it. He's a very good tap dancer. He does it because he wants an outlet for something. People love it; they're rabid about it. I was in vaudeville years ago, but right now I have more fun teaching than I did actually dancing.

—**Jack Epply**
tap instructor
Atlanta, Georgia

Surprisingly, the amateurs are sometimes better natural entertainers than the professionals. For the instructor who is used to a studio full of grim, determined students, the amateur boom is making tap class an exciting and unpredictable arena. The teachers are having a ball, too.

I had a girl who literally screwed herself to the stage one night. The routine ended with *piqué* turns—which is a ballet term for a turn done on one foot—and the screw in her tap shoe had worked itself loose and also the head had broken off the screw. Apparently, she was doing the turns in a countermotion to how the screw had gone in—that's the only thing I can figure out—and after about three turns she literally screwed herself to the floor. She couldn't get out and she had to take her shoe off. The audience roared.

—**Beverly Rudman**
tap instructor
Minneapolis, Minnesota

There is yet another side to the re-emergence of tap dancing. Amateur tappers refer to a larger impetus, a wholly separate motivation for undertaking the activity.

Actually, I do it to get off my feet. I've had bone spurs in my heels and I've been wearing a support for about three years now, so it was almost on doctor's orders that I took it up, because I would be using a whole new set of muscles. It's surprising, getting into a pair of tap shoes and going through

the routines—at the end of a half hour it was marvelous. With the relaxation of those muscles I'd been using all day, I'd feel it in my ankles and in the balls of my feet, instead of that burning sensation. It feels good. It's therapy for my feet.

—**Jerry Teener**
amateur tapper
Minneapolis, Minnesota

Amateurs claim that there are distinct physical benefits to be derived from tap dancing, and many dance instructors support this claim. Back in the good old days, tap dancing was like getting your first pair of long pants or starting to shave. It was just another part of growing up.

I've got lots of kids who come in because their parents feel that tap is a necessary part of their education. They've got to have it for coordination, personality development, and body control. People think just ballet and jazz do that, but there's a great deal to be said for tap.

—**Al Gilbert**

For those who forgot to grow up, or for some reason missed out on the fun, adults can use tap dancing to start from scratch.

Quite frankly, if somebody had not been physically inclined at all, didn't do gymnastics, wasn't active in sports in school, didn't play tennis, didn't ride bicycles, was strictly a desk-type person, I would probably say go to tap first.

—**Gwen Bowen**
tap instructor
Denver, Colorado

16

One of the most frequently cited reasons people give for taking up tap is that it's great physical exercise. Tap makes you healthy; it's good for the heart, the blood, the muscles, the lungs. With the re-emergence of tap as an art form, people have also seized upon the dance to get back in shape: to improve their stamina, to slim down the thighs, firm up the buttocks, put some grace into the arms, some line to the neck, some ease to the skull, and some tousle to the hair. There are more than enough reasons.

> They talk about jogging, but to me it's a lot more fun to tap, and you get just as winded if you go for an hour. It's mostly in the breathing and maybe the heartbeat. Very definitely.
> —Jacqueline Jensen

While tap dancing is not a panacea or cure-all, there is unanimous agreement that tap is first-rate physical exercise. Wait, better make that *nearly* unanimous agreement:

> It's exceedingly hard to learn to tap dance, but it's not exercise at all if you haven't learned it. If you're going to do it to lose weight, you wouldn't be able to do it hard enough to lose weight for about ten years. Out of my experience, that's all I can say. If you just like to hop around to music, that's something else again, but you're not going to lose weight doing it. You're not going to get in shape and, as far as I know, you won't even be able to work up a sweat.
> —**Paul Draper**
> tap professional; developer of
> the concert balletic style of tap
> dancing to classical music
> Pittsburgh, Pennsylvania

Is Draper right? Could the entire argument for the health benefits of tap dancing be simply a load of amateur mumbo-jumbo? A leading dance critic and social commentator makes a serious charge that offers a possible explanation for today's physical glorification of tap dancing:

> Nobody ever does it for the exercise. That's a rationalization to cover up their fantasies. Look, everybody wants to be Shirley Temple, right? It's the fulfillment of a childish fantasy. Those Shirley Temple movies are on television all the time. It's a form of infantilism—you know, people want to be stars. But it's a harmless infantilism and a harmless fantasizing, because tap dancing gives you pleasure, but surely the underlying psychological thing is wanting to be a star.
> —**Patrick O'Connor**
> dance and drama critic
> New York, New York

Are tappers deluding themselves? Could it be that people's claims for the health benefits of tap are covering up their true reasons? Is the whole thing based on a fantasy of fulfilling the secret ambition to be another Fred Astaire or Eleanor Powell—at least for their friends? Perhaps, but even amateur tappers experience occasional moments of glory, becoming instant stars with a clever shuffle as onlookers turn and admire.

17

There are professionals who take a skeptical view of all this amateur activity.

> I don't think there is a tap revival. I've only seen one sign in some national magazine—I don't know whether it was *Time* or *Newsweek*. It said there was a revival in tap dancing and that the reason for the revival was because it was so easy to learn—you could learn to tap dance in about twenty minutes. I've been trying to learn to tap dance for about thirty-five years and I haven't learned how yet. I don't know what all these people are doing, but it is not tap dancing.
>
> **—Paul Draper**

From a professional standpoint, Draper may be right. Tap clearly has a way to go before it can be regarded as a full-fledged part of modern show business, and we will explore some of the reasons for this in a later chapter. Yet, as we have tried to suggest, ordinary Americans have indeed rediscovered tap as a new leisure activity. As of this writing, enrollment in amateur tap classes has visibly increased around the country—and who among us can say with certainty that somewhere, in some dim studio, practicing feverishly, there is not a new Cagney, Keeler, or Kelly? But whatever they are doing, these amateur tappers take it seriously and, in small but significant ways, make their contribution to the state of the art.

> I wish they'd make better shoes. I don't like my tap shoes. I think I could do a lot better if I had some good tap shoes. They're not comfortable and the heels are up, so that means the balls of your feet are down. They're not cushioned very well, and that means the balls of your feet get sore. And the taps fall off and my strap is splitting. I mean, I just think they could do better. Tell them to do better. Write that.
>
> **—Lisa Bradley**

CHAPTER TWO

ℰWhy Tap?

People don't really know what tap dancing is. All they know is that they put some taps on their shoes, jump out, and hit some steps and do some sound, but they don't really know what tap dancing is.
—**Sandman Sims**
professional tap dancer; known for his dance on sand, featured in *Tap Happening* (1969) and *The Hoofers* (1969)
New York, New York

Dancing seems to satisfy a basic need. There is something inside each of us that wants to work its way out in this distinctly human manner.

For some crazy reason this need to move seems to be concentrated in the impatience of the leg. The way the physiognomy of the human being exists, a good deal of that restlessness emanates in the foot. This is indigenous to the neuromuscular system of the individual.
—**Murray Louis**
modern dancer and founder of the Murray Louis Dance Company
New York, New York

Dance turns this restlessness into rhythm, giving that impulse to move a form of self-expression in which the human body moving in time and space becomes the medium, a living work of art.

Appreciate this gift of dance. With minimal apparatus and ornamentation, dance frees the artist from the material requirements that go along with other art forms. In dance, there are no paints to dry up, no strings to go out of tune, no marble blocks to crack and crumble, no ambiguous words to punctuate—there is only the human body and the ground. The simplicity is exquisite. The impact, stunning.

From the beginning, we have had this urge to move and this opportunity to create. In recent years, owing in part to jazz and the liberating influences of the sixties, ordinary people have rediscovered body movement and dance as means for individual expression.

> As human beings, we always must dance. It's a thing that's very deep; it's in the blood. Within the last fifteen years, I think people have come to realize this. People have felt their bodies freed somewhat, and suddenly they respect their own individuality. It's a time of awareness. People are starting to take note of themselves and look at what's really important.
>
> **—Todd Bolender**
> ballet choreographer and former
> premier dancer of major ballet
> companies
> New York, New York

But what is special about *tap* dance? What distinguishes it from the other forms of dance? What *is* tap dancing, anyway?

Tap dancing is *sound*—the music of rhythmic sound made with the feet. Tap is the dance form that combines sight and sound. Aside from flamenco, every other dance form offers only something to look at, movement to observe; but in tap dancing there is also something to hear.

Everything else follows from this. The tapper fixes metal plates, the taps, to the toe and heel of each shoe. By skillfully manipulating these taps against a hard floor, the dancer can produce a wide range of sounds. Depending on which tap is hit, where and how hard, the tapper can traverse a scale of musical sounds beneath his or her feet.

> I can duplicate any kind of sound I hear. I can do it with my feet. It's an ear thing; you hear it and you can do it.
>
> **—Sandman Sims**

With this instrument the tapper stands apart from all other dancers. Part of the dancer's skill can be ascertained in the intricacy of the sound patterns he or she produces. The tap dancer is a drummer, too.

> It's very important that people be made aware that it's not just putting taps on your shoes. Tap is a certain form of dancing in which rhythm is the basic ingredient. Rhythm and sound added to movement is an addition over what other dancing does. All other dancing is strictly visual.
>
> **—Jack Stanly**
> one of the nation's leading tap
> instructors
> Miami, Florida

Tap lets you make lovely noise. Some people who do not consider themselves artists do it solely for this reason—they want to be heard. They

Two generations of former Radio City Music Hall Rockettes:
Jeanne Remy and daughter Carrie Evers.

want to blast out and express themselves in a blatant racket. They want to
fight back against the roar of jets, the boom of factories, the whirr of air
conditioners, the slamming of doors, the battering of jackhammers, the
car horns, doorbells, telephones, stereos, barking dogs, alarm clocks, scream-
ing babies, ambulance sirens, whistling teakettles, banging garbage can
lids . . . and dripping faucets in the night.

But for the performer, that "noise" is transformed into a work of art,
an aesthetic means of reaching other people.

21

I was discussing it with my daughter Carrie—she's a former Rockette, too—
and I asked her, "Why do you think it's coming back?" She said, "Jazz is
an expression of yourself, too, but a lot of people do not have the ability to
move their bodies the way jazz should be performed. I think in tap dancing
you can communicate with other people. You can hear that what you are
thinking inside is coming out of your feet."

> —**Jeanne Remy**
> tap instructor and former
> member of the Radio City
> Music Hall Rockettes
> Verona, New Jersey

Because the object in tap dancing is as much sound as sight, you
get instant feedback on your performance, you can attempt a step and use
your ears to tell you if you've done it right. You can monitor the position,

The Nicholas Brothers: Fayard (*left*) and Harold (*right*), performing an exciting leap from which they often landed in a split.

the motion, and the force of the step by listening to the music you create. For this reason, tap may be especially well suited for an amateur. As with any dance, you can judge your progress in the mirror, but with tap you can also evaluate it in your ears.

It is no coincidence that tap dancing is coming back at this moment in our culture. Tap is ecologically efficient; it satisfies several of our senses at once.

Moreover, because tap is *structured* dancing, it may be satisfying the same need for form that can be seen in the return to the more structured social dances. When you tap dance, you don't just learn steps, you learn to combine them in an ordered sequence of distinct rhythmic motions. It requires effort and discipline to learn these complex movements, yet the very difficulty of it seems to evoke determined interest. It is a challenge that rewards us with the lovely music of our shoes.

> Now there you are, people want to tap dance today because they're not as lazy as they used to be. I remember when I first started teaching in the sixties, a lot of students would come to see what was happening and they would say, "We're going to do that." But then the following week I didn't have as many. They didn't want to work at it then. But today, my goodness, I can't handle all the kids that are coming now. There are so many of them and they all have the energy now. There's been a change in the country. It's something new. People are noticing tap and saying, "This is an American art. We should be doing this, too."
>
> —**Fayard Nicholas**
> half of the famous Nicholas
> Brothers dance team of stage and
> screen
> Los Angeles, California

> I tried from the time I was six until the time I was eighteen, and my father kept saying, "Only fairies tap dance." And I said, "What about your friend Gene Kelly?" And he said, "He's different."
> —**Patrick O'Connor**

For many people, the appeal of tap lies in the images of its most famous practitioners. On film, Fred Astaire and Gene Kelly epitomized *cool* and *suave,* a stylish and vigorous manliness. Women tappers such as Eleanor Powell and Ann Miller projected a sense of independence and control, but without compromising their femininity; they alway remained confident of their dance steps and their womanhood.

The lure of tap dancing goes far beyond these sex-role images, however. It goes back to the period of tap's heyday, that time about a generation ago when tap dancing was *the* dance of American musical comedy. The renewed interest in tap is also an attempt to restore some sense of that exciting, vibrant period.

> The great tap period was an era that embodied class and style. So much of that has been lost today, and people are looking for things that will bring about some sort of elegance, some sense of style. The people who are trying to

Buster Brown, a featured tap dancer with Duke Ellington's band,
later one of The Hoofers, "dances the pressure right off him."
James J. Kriegsmann.

learn tap dancing now are not so much capturing what they did with the taps, but recapturing the style of it.

—**George Faison**
modern and jazz dancer;
choreographer of *The Wiz*
New York, New York

Tap offers a return to "style," a moment's contact with the happy, healthy, elegant atmosphere of America's glamorous past. But this effort to retrieve the past represents more than another nostalgia boom; the attraction links up with our renewed dedication in the seventies. Today, Americans are a disillusioned people, trying to salvage something of value from our no-longer-innocent heritage. In recent years appalling disclosures have shattered many of the myths upon which this country's prestige and self-respect had rested. With each new glimpse of the actual forces behind our politics and diplomacy, we are called upon to question our integrity as a nation.

It is natural under such conditions that Americans should seek a remnant of that powerful image American cinema has projected around the world. In its small but perhaps significant way, the tap tradition evokes that image of down-to-earth sophistication, morality, and lightheartedness that Americans once cherished as themselves. With good reason, people are looking

Dancing the Irish jig, about 1894. A good way to keep warm—skillful step dancers could execute as many as fifteen taps per second.
The Bettmann Archive.

to tap, hoping to find some aspect of that great American myth that may remain intact today. Through tap, you put yourself in touch with an older vision of America. And by trying it yourself, by going through the motions that you've watched so many times before, you give yourself an opportunity to experience for yourself a sense of the carefree elegance that was formerly confined to stage and screen.

Even professional tappers will tell you that tap dancing has its elements of myth and fantasy. Tap is visual, vocal, and it attracts attention. It can serve the personal motives of a make-believe Shirley Temple or the international goals of America the Beautiful. But whatever your expressed interest in tap—be it noise-making or nostalgia, structure or style, exercise or ecstasy—one undeniably simple benefit overrides all the fancy theories and excuses. When all is said and done, there's only one real reason why you can't beat tap dancing: It makes you happy.

Tap dancing has no messages; it leaves those to Western Union. It's not trying to solve the problems of the world through tragedy. It shows us how to have fun. It certainly does. You never saw a sad tap dancer.

—Jack Stanly

Tap dancers have something going that a lot of people don't have going. When we have problems, it seems it's easier for us to go into a little room, or go anyplace, wherever you are, and just dance it off, dance it right away. I was talking to Tony Condos and he said the same thing. He said, "Man, we can get over things." Even if you don't have a record player, you can just create your own sounds in your mind and dance a lot of things away. I guess a lot of singers can sing their troubles away, but I think a dancer can do it easier than anybody. He can just dance the pressure right off him.

—Buster Brown
tap dancer featured in Duke
Ellington's band and *The Hoofers*
New York, New York

CHAPTER THREE

An American Tap-istry

Every culture has a dance of some kind that can be said to be a fore-runner of tap. Centuries ago, the Dutch were already clopping back and forth across the dikes in their wooden shoes; the Cossacks were kicking over the Steppes in leather boots; and African tribes were pounding the hard, dry earth in their bare feet.

Most ethnic folk dances contain elements that can be likened to tap, but tap dancing as we know it today is a uniquely American product. Although it has identifiable roots in certain dances of Europe and Africa, tap dancing, like most American creations, is the result of a blending of cultures—a melting-pot fusion of old-world traditions with new-world imagination to create a new dance that expressed our unique American spirit.

Early dance historians tried to trace the development of tap as a linear progression from a single ethnic source, giving an incomplete, albeit neat and simple, picture of tap dancing. Rare journals from the plantation days of early American slavery make reference to the first Negro contributions to dance forms that gradually developed into tap, and various books on the minstrel era or the days of vaudeville touch briefly upon important European figures in the development of the form. It was not until the 1930s that we began to understand the complex origins of tap dancing, in several books on tap as physical education, published by A. S. Barnes and Company, that traced the dance to both black and white sources.

Today, by far the best work on the black man's role in the evolution of tap dancing is the late Marshall Stearns's monumental treatise, *Jazz Dance,*

An antique post-
card pose of the
Duncan Brothers, a
famous clog dance
team from the ear-
liest days of vaude-
ville.
*New York Public
Library at Lincoln
Center, Dance Col-
lection.*

which comprehensively researches and connects tap dancing to that aspect
of what Stearns calls "vernacular dance" performed specifically to jazz
music. Published by Macmillan and Company in 1968, *Jazz Dance* contains
astute analysis and primary source material that was of invaluable assist-
ance to us in putting together this history.

In telling the story of tap, we've attempted to avoid massive encyclopedic
detail—this has been done elsewhere. Instead, we've chosen to concentrate
on the most important scenes in the tap'istry, highlighting the key figures
and innovations and providing, we hope, some of the flavor of the cultural
influences that come together in this lively, happy dance.

The Granddaddy of Tap Dancing

The year is 466. St. Patrick is tromping through the gooey bogs of Ireland. In villages and tribes around the island, his pagan flock are already
performing lively "step dances," the first forms of the Irish jig, grand
progenitor of the ancestral line of tap.

The early Irish peasants wore hard shoes, footwear designed for protection against the year-round inclement weather of the British Isles. Maybe to keep warm, maybe to amuse themselves, maybe for no reason whatsoever, the inhabitants of Ireland developed their jig, a distinctive step dance in which the dancer's main preoccupation was with intricate leg movement and footwork. Tapping was done with both the toes and heels, while the dancer held his arms close to his sides, keeping the upper half of his body erect and nearly motionless. In order to concentrate fully on their feet, the Irish step dancers gave no thought to such dance characteristics as overall body line or facial expression. The dancing was fast and involved, with skillful step dancers executing as many as fifteen taps in one second. So it was that in Ireland long ago the human body was transformed into a musical instrument, bringing forth rhythmic "shoe music."

Tap Shoe Music

Across the Irish Sea, in England, footwork was taking a turn of its own, so that by the mid-1700s step dancing began to take on the competitive characteristics which made innovation, and hence *improvisation*, synonymous with the dance itself.

In the manufacturing city of Lancashire, the dawning hours of the Industrial Revolution found the local workers suffering under appalling factory conditions. In addition to the normal chilling dampness of the region, the introduction of the steam engine and the growth of the iron foundries produced working environments fit only for blisters and consumption. In self-defense, workers began to wear shoes with soles and heels cut out of one piece of solid, insulating wood. They called these shoes "clogs."

During recreation periods the men and women would dance on the stone streets outside of the mills. Contests were held to see who could produce the most varied sounds and rhythms. Competition was fierce but good-natured, and the favored steps were eventually integrated into the British folk dance known as the Lancashire Clog. As with the Irish jigs and reels, British clog dancing was distinctive shoe music. Upper body movement was eliminated as dancers beat out many of the steps that were soon to emigrate to the American stage.

As the dances developed, tempos got faster and steps became more intricate; and, as a result, the wooden soles of the British clog dancers proved awkward and even dangerous. By the early 1800s the dancers' wooden soles were replaced by more flexible leather soles, and English copper pennies were screwed on the heels of the shoes in order to emphasize the sound. The quality of this new sound had an attraction of its own, and eventually the coinage was replaced by metal toe-tips, called "taps." With this, real "tap dancing" was born, and shoe music came into its own as a form of entertainment.

African tribesmen performing a ritual stomp dance from the film
Savage Splendor.
New York Public Library at Lincoln Center, Dance Collection.

African natives dancing, 1928.
New York Public Library at Lincoln Center, Dance Collection.

Meanwhile in Africa

Tribal Africans danced with their whole bodies, not just with their feet. Shoeless on the bare earth, the sounds produced by the black dancers' feet were barely audible. Instead, African tribesmen concentrated on generating vivid body movements and originating rhythms unique to their individual tribes. The entire body was thrown into motion. In direct contrast to the European step dancers, the degree of skill depended upon the dancers' ability to bend, crouch, and flex with agility and decorum.

To early white observers, the deep, pounding rhythms of African music lent to its dances a wild and frenzied character; but the various tribal dances were actually highly structured, moving outward from the hips and employing the rest of the body and extremities according to the specific rituals of each tribe. Pygmy dancers developed their own distinctive footwork; the Congolese concentrated on further inflections of the hip and loin; the Dahomean tribesmen focused on movement of the head and shoulders. Within their particular forms, however, African dances called for constant improvisation. Dancers were free to imitate animals, develop their own individual themes, and shape the dance however the spirit prompted.

In all African dances, however, movement was almost completely flat-footed. Because there was virtually no sound and little delineation of the toe and heel movement as in Europe, African dance really had little to do with the early art of tap. The African steps consisted of gliding, dragging, or shuffling while the body was kept flexible and at ease. It wasn't until the sophisticated beat of the African dances encountered the already highly developed European shoe music that the blending of footwork and syncopation became possible.

The Collision of Cultures

What we now recognize as American tap dancing had its beginning when the start of the slave trade in the New World brought about the first collision of European and African cultures. During the long sea voyage from Africa to the Americas, the newly captive slaves were brought up on deck to exercise and entertain the crew. When weather permitted, to keep their cargo healthy, the European crewmen forced the slaves to dance on the wooden decks. For their own vigor as well, crewmen did their native step dances for the benefit of their first black audiences.

Here, in the middle of the Atlantic, practitioners of these two very different dance forms viewed each other for the first time. By the time the slave ships reached the New World, the sight and sound of the different races' steps and rhythms had prepared the way for the blending of dances that followed.

Tap and Slavery

The initial merging of cultures that produced American tap dancing was far from wholly amicable. In the colonies, the politics of slavery found the Africans holding fast to their native traditions. In 1739, in Stono, Virginia, a group of slaves planning a revolt beat out a message on drums to alert slaves at neighboring plantations. The Stono slave insurrection was put down, and the next year brought the passage of the Slave Act of 1740, which prohibited American Negro slaves from "beating drums, blowing horns or the like." Having lost the right to use any musical instruments that might emit a warning sound, the slaves substituted handclaps and footbeats, more for enjoyment than for communication between planta-

Thomas Dartmouth Rice as Jumping Jim Crow, 1836
New York Public Library at Lincoln Center, Theater Collection.

tions. In this manner they created their own form of music, one where the dancer was responsible for creating his own rhythm and sound. The new "body music" of the slaves would make them especially responsive to the new entertainers who had just arrived in the North, bringing with them the improvisational shoe music of Europe.

The Africans first applied their rhythms to European dances on the plantations. As on shipboard, the white masters of the Old South often made their plantation slaves perform for them. To stimulate greater enthusiasm, a prize of a cake was offered to the slave who could perform the fanciest walk along a straight line in front of his white audience. Slaves used this opportunity to parody the high manners of the white folks' parties, where the guests danced the elegant grand march of the Minuet. The slaves would parade in a mock march, with heads high, chins up, and noses in the air. In this fashion, the notorious Cakewalk succeeded in entertaining members of both races. From the success of the satire, one wonders if the folks in the big house didn't miss the point entirely, marveling instead at the ingenuity of their slave crews. Later slave dances copied the stiff bodies and flying feet of the Irish jig dancers from the North, who in the early 1800s paid frequent visits to the southern estates.

The First Minstrels

During the summer of 1828, N. M. Ludlow's theater company was spending the summer in Louisville, Kentucky. Between performances, the entertainers entertained themselves by watching the pathetic but amusing walk of the old slave who tended the livery stable behind the theater. One professional dancer, a white man named Thomas Dartmouth Rice, became keenly interested in the twisted gait of old Daddy, who, like most slaves, was named after his owner, Jim Crow. Crow suffered from a deformed right shoulder, a stiff left leg bent at the knee, and a bad limp. As he tottered around the yard he would sing a little song he had composed, and at the end of each verse he would give a crippled jump and come down on his heel, singing:

> *Wheel about, turn about,*
> *Do jis so,*
> *An, ebery time I wheel about,*
> *I jump Jim Crow.*

Rice observed Jim Crow's distorted dance. He wrote down a few verses of his own and upped the pace a bit, then he borrowed a set of porter's clothes, blackened his face with burnt cork, and performed Jim Crow's song and dance for the Louisville audience out front. The act was an instant hit. Rice was called back for twenty curtain calls on the first night, and American minstrelsy had the blackface prototype it was soon to develop into an international craze.

Jumping Jim Crow became a popular social dance of its day, and minstrelsy spread across the country like wildfire as white entertainers donned burnt cork and worked up their own imitations of the antics of slavery. In 1843, seasoned minstrel musicians Whitlock, Pelham, Brower, and Emmett came together in Whitlock's boarding house in New York City. The four performers picked up their instruments—fiddle, banjo, bones, and tambourine—and held a jam session that turned out to be the premier gathering of America's first minstrel group, the Virginia Minstrels. On February 6, 1843, with Emmett's classic "Old Dan Tucker" as their lead tune, the Virginia Minstrels opened in blackface at the Bowery Amphitheatre. The minstrel group was an immediate success, and the Virginia Minstrels soon greeted competition from the Christy Minstrels, Bryant's Minstrels, and the host of other imitators who followed.

The Melting Pot

Black slaves continued to parody their masters and white minstrels stole the mannerisms of the Negro until, finally, in the 1840s, New York City offered an opportunity for a fair exchange of white and black dancing talent. Newly freed slaves and recently arrived Irish immigrants met on equal footing in the Five Points district of New York around the area then called Paradise Square (today the intersection of Baxter, Worth, and Park streets in lower Manhattan). In the brothels and saloons around Paradise Square, white and black dancers first traded Irish jig steps for African rhythms. Here, too, the Lancashire tradition of dance challenge was imported, with great promotion, for the legendary confrontations between an Irishman, John Diamond, and a black man, William Henry Lane, also known as Juba, "King of All Dancers."

A free-born Negro, Juba learned to dance from "Uncle" Jim Lowe, a black jig-and-reel dancer who, in the tradition of early minstrelsy, was not allowed to perform in white theaters. Presenting his original fusion of European steps and African rhythms, Juba became the only black dancer to be accepted by the early white minstrel companies. Moreover, his clear superiority as a dancer brought him top billing when performing with white companies. In 1844, Juba and Diamond, generally acclaimed to be the greatest white jig dancer, held a series of contests, which formalized the challenge match and established the custom of using three sets of judges to referee a tap dancing competition. Overall-style judges observed the dancers from the orchestra pit; single-minded time judges watched the contestants from the wings; and keen-eared step judges made their decisions from under the stage based on the quality of the sound alone.

Amidst a field of white imitators, Juba was the major black dancer of the minstrel era. In 1848, he joined Pell's Ethiopian Serenaders in London and gained a reputation throughout Europe as the only authentic master of the African-American style of dance.

The Soft Shoe

Europeans continued to enter America in great waves as conditions on

Black dancers perform a wild barroom dance in a Western scene from Dickens' *American Notes*.
The Bettmann Archive.

Flyer for J. W. Brown's *Rabbit Foot Minstrels.*
New York Public Library at Lincoln Center, Theater Collection.

35

the Continent prompted the emigration of other nationalities besides the Irish and English. A wave of German immigrants after the German wars of 1847 brought with them folk dances of their own, such as the Bavarian *Shuhplatteltanz*, the *Schottische*, the polka, and the waltz. In the United States, the melting pot produced a German-Irish waltz clog, a step dance in ¾ time, which was the forerunner of the graceful soft shoe of the song and dance men.

On the minstrel stage, the waltz clog was naturalized into the famed Essence of Old Virginia, an American version based on the slow-tempoed shuffle of the old plantation blacks. White minstrels like Dan Bryant and Eddie Girard glided gracefully across the stage, and the black minstrel Billy Kersands became famous for his rendition of "Wait Till the Clouds Roll By," in which he would strip off a dozen vests as he sang and danced the Essence. In this period, too, Barney Fagan, an Irish clog dancer, first presented a syncopated version of the Irish jig, while clog dancing experimented with swinging rhythm in other performances by white minstrels such as Lew Dockstader, George Wilson, and George Gorman.

The Essence matured into the more controlled and refined soft shoe when George Primrose, a Canadian of Irish ancestry, traded his clogs for leather soles. Primrose, the Fred Astaire of his day, performed a cool, effortless soft shoe that influenced every dancer in minstrelsy and vaudeville. He toured with major minstrel companies—McFarland's Minstrels, O'Brien's Circus, and Haverly's Mastodon Minstrels—before he teamed up with William H. West to form Primrose and West Minstrels. Primrose made the transition into vaudeville and maintained his status as master of the soft shoe well into the 1900s.

The Death of Minstrelsy

The Civil War brought an end to the black-white challenges as competition between the races ceased to be a matter for national entertainment. With the legislating of racial equality, the competition moved into a political arena—free white versus free black—and the basic premise of the minstrel parody lost a bit of its magic charm. After the war, carpetbaggers, segregationists, and other antebellum celebrities greased the skids of minstrelsy's special form of racism, setting the scene for the decline of the big-time shows.

Other shortcomings of the form became apparent about the time of the Civil War, as women first became accepted as popular entertainers in the United States. A talented Irishwoman, Kitty O'Neill, became one of the country's first great woman entertainers, holding her own with a sand dance—a noisy, hard-soled soft shoe—that made her a match for Primrose, Eddie Leonard, and other popular male entertainers of the day. Clearly, though, minstrelsy was no place for women. Female performers didn't fit in comfortably with the medicine shows, the gilly truck stages, or the carnival tents.

The renowned George Primrose and his Cotton Coons Minstrel
Company.
New York Public Library at Lincoln Center, Theater Collection.

The Royce Sisters, early
women vaudeville danc-
ers, performing a strut
and waving top hats.
*New York Public Library
at Lincoln Center, Dance
Collection.*

Two legends from white minstrelsy and vaudeville: George Primrose (*left*) and Lew Dockstader, about 1900.
New York Public Library at Lincoln Center, Theater Collection.

The introduction of women into minstrelsy helped crumble its rigid structure. As the nation pulled out of its dark age of civil strife, masculine musical comedy based on white male supremacy left something to be desired; and audiences looked for a new form of entertainment, one with more variety and sex appeal. They found it in the new concept of "family entertainment," which was introduced in vaudeville.

Tap dancing moved forward with great vigor in vaudeville, continuing its haphazard evolution in two separate arenas. Black and white entertainment were kept apart, heading down dual paths of development that rarely intersected in performance. In this era, the great names of black and white vaudeville form a twin chain of dancers, comprising a sort of double helix that winds around the core of tap without ever joining into a single strand.

White Vaudeville

A white man from New Jersey gave vaudeville its start as family entertainment that offered more than any minstrel show. In 1881, Tony Pastor premiered a tasteful presentation at the 14th Street Theater in New York with a broadened performance consisting of eight acts of comedy, acrobatics, song, and dance, with an inoffensive sprinkling of topical humor and light entertainment. Vaudeville became even bigger than minstrelsy. The biggest theaters, such as the Palace in New York, hosted two shows a day well into the 1930s.

In white vaudeville, it was a time of spectacular invention. Tom Patricola, one of the most famous early names, contributed original steps and played the ukelele as he danced. He also developed a new sort of blackface imitation mimicking urban types such as icemen and baggagemen. The legendary Pat Rooney, known for his waltz clog, is also credited with popularizing two of the most famous tap steps. In Off to Buffalo, the classic exit step, Rooney's hands pumped up and down and one foot stepped high as he moved offstage with an "away we go!" look. In Falling Off a Log, Rooney spun one foot in front of the other with a controlled, rolling appearance. In vaudeville's early days, Irishman Eddie Horan was said to be the first to dance the walking waltz clog with a cane, a routine that soon became a standard in nearly every song and dance act.

One of the most intriguing competitions in vaudeville was not between dancers but, rather, historians who tried to pin down who invented what and when. Foremost among the controversies was deciding on the originator of the Stair Dance, that impressive dance trip up and down a flight of stairs, which was later immortalized by Bill Robinson. During the 1880s, credit for the first Stair Dance was given to Eddie Mack, Al Leach, and a woman performer, Margie Trainor, with others, no doubt, claiming the innovation since.

Around the turn of the century, white vaudevillians added new flair and power to comedy dancing. Irishmen Harry Kelly and John T. Kennedy introduced the first very fast tap steps, a feat soon bested by the famous Condos Brothers, who perfected a lightning-fast maneuver called the Five Tap Wing, a step in which the dancer leaps on one foot and makes a series of tap sounds on the floor while still in the air. The Condos Brothers gained fame for their ability to execute five distinct sounds in rhythm, incorporating this feature into the general body movement of the dance.

The names roll by in the later years of white vaudeville as renowned dancers, teams, and specialty acts took their cues and bowed at the waist. One of the most versatile white dancers, James Barton, began his career as a burlesque comedian by observing and imitating the popular rubber-leg movements of the black dancers. Harland Dixon, a prominent character dancer and half of the famous team of Doyle and Dixon, was said to be able to pantomime anybody or anything. There was the great George M.

Famous vaudevillians James P. Doyle (*left*) and Harland Dixon, 1916.
Fred Kelly.

Cohan, author, playwright, actor, singer, and dancer, who began his career in vaudeville as the youngest of the Four Cohans in 1889. Cohan's first professional tap dance was called The Lively Bootblack, in which young George performed his own parody of the black style of dancing known as Buck and Wing, a bright, fast-tempoed tap dance.

Along the T.O.B.A. Circuit

The world of black vaudeville existed in a phantom dimension alongside the established showcases of white entertainment. Just before the first World War, Sherman Dudley, a black comedian from Washington, D.C., began leasing and purchasing theaters and contacting theater owners throughout the South and Southwest. The network they formed was called the Theater Owners' Booking Association, T.O.B.A., which was nicknamed "Tough On Black Artists" or just called "Toby" for short. By the 1920s, T.O.B.A. covered black entertainment markets in most of the South and many northern cities, at its peak connecting over three hundred theaters. Along the T.O.B.A. circuit, black performers found an audience and an arena in which to develop their own style of tap dancing.

Few T.O.B.A. acts ever gained nationwide recognition from the white entertainment world, but most of the black entertainers who later came to the attention of white audiences got their start through Toby. These include such legendary acts as the Berry Brothers, an acrobatic team, and the Whitman Sisters, one of the leading family acts of black vaudeville. From about 1900, May, Essie, Alberta, and Alice Whitman ran their own show and maintained a touring company that headlined for more than forty years.

Competition was fierce along the T.O.B.A. circuit, and performers had to tap their greatest resources of energy and imagination. Because of this vitality, and because new developments on Broadway and in Hollywood were slower to make an impact on black entertainment, T.O.B.A. was still going strong when white vaudeville was already in decline. In T.O.B.A., tap dancing reached its highest level yet of inherent sophistication, combining the steps, props, and styles of white vaudeville with the special rhythms and personalities of numerous black innovators.

King Rastus Brown remains one of the early unsung heroes of black tap dancing. A master of the flat-footed hoofing style, Brown was known primarily among black entertainers for his masterful Buck dancing, the earliest combination of the basic shuffle and tap steps. Buck dancing was the first American tap performed to syncopated rhythms, a fundamental characteristic of all jazz music in which the accents are placed not on the straight beat, as with the jigs, clogs, and other dances of European origin, but on the "downbeat" or "offbeat," a style derived primarily from the rhythms of African tribal music. Brown was the king of Buck dancing in his day, but he lacked the comedic skills required of popular entertainers and never achieved recognition from either white or black audiences.

Grace and Eddie Rector, about 1920. He is considered one of the
all-time greats.
The Helen Armstead-Johnson Foundation for Theater Research.

Among black tappers, Eddie Rector is recognized as the first to give the art a measure of elegance and grace through a more integrated and fluid body motion. Rector started as a soft-shoe performer and then developed his own style. He incorporated hand and arm movements with a traveling pace, a departure from the black hoofing tradition in which dancers stayed in one place and concentrated solely on footwork.

Following the first major appearance of T.O.B.A. performers on Broadway in *Shuffle Along* (1921), black precision dancers adopted Rector's style in the first black "class act." Until the twenties, blacks had always played slow-witted, shiftless types, usually seen on stage in a pair of tattered overalls, shooting craps, stealing chickens, and eating watermelon underneath a shady theatrical tree. In *Liza* (1922), the team of Rufus Greenlee and Thaddeus Drayton became the first black dancers to appear on Broadway wearing monocles, top hats, and tails, at last breaking free of the old stereotyped roles.

Perhaps one of black vaudeville's best all-round entertainers, and one of its most impressive innovators, was John W. Bubbles. At age ten he teamed up with pianist Ford Lee "Buck" Washington, who was then six, to form Buck and Bubbles, black tapping's most famous song and dance team. In 1922, Bubbles created a new style of tap dancing, which he called Rhythm Tap, a casual but complex, highly syncopated style of tapping performed at half the tempo of most other black dancing of its day. Bubbles's deceptively nonchalant manner led to the introduction and refinement of a skillful, dignified tap style. Bubbles would incorporate into his easy style extra tap sounds and unusual accents by dropping his heels, clicking his toes together, and adding rhythmic turns and combinations to his relaxed "traveling" pace. Bubbles was a hit in the *Ziegfeld Follies of 1931*, and he went on to play the role of Sportin' Life at the request of composer George Gershwin in *Porgy and Bess* (1935). Later, in Hollywood, he made several movies, including *A Song Is Born* (1947), with Judy Garland.

Without a doubt, the unrivaled king of black tap dancing was Bill Robinson, the legendary Mr. Bojangles, who was in every way a master and a star. He achieved notoriety in minstrel shows, vaudeville, and on Broadway before traveling to Hollywood, where he became one of the first black superstars of Hollywood's golden era.

Born in 1878 in Richmond, Virginia, Robinson began touring at the age of twelve with a minstrel show called *The South Before the War*, which featured the white soft-shoe specialist Eddie Leonard. Bojangles—the name comes from "bone jangler," a musician who beats out rhythm by knocking a pair of bones together—was heavily influenced by white dancers like Leonard, James Barton, Jack Donahue, and George Primrose, but he eventually joined the T.O.B.A. circuit and later emerged on Broadway in Lew Leslie's revue, *The Blackbirds*. Robinson's adept, syncopated waltz clog was performed up on the toes, with little arm or body motion but an

John Bubbles of "Buck and Bubbles." A master of the "free and easy" style, he performed highly difficult footwork with seemingly casual ease.

easy swinging style that complimented his perfectly controlled footwork.

Bill Robinson became the first black dancer to headline a show of his own on Broadway, *Brown Buddies* (1930). In 1932, he went west to Hollywood, where he teamed up with young Shirley Temple, whom he coached and first co-starred with in *The Little Colonel* (1935). In *The Littlest Rebel* (1935), Robinson and Temple performed a gala version of the Stair Dance that Robinson made famous in vaudeville. In all, he made fourteen films in Hollywood (see Chapter Four).

The Great Revues

The turning of the century saw the beginning of the American chorus line and the rise of the extravagant Broadway revues, which made tap dancing an American institution. The great revues offered tap dancing a first-class showcase that made the dance form synonymous with the glamor and electricity of the American stage.

Synchronized tap dancing started with the famous Florodora Girls of 1900, the Yama-yama Girls of 1905, and Ned Wayburn's Minstrel Misses of 1906, as American audiences discovered the vital element of sex appeal that was totally absent in minstrel dancing and only dawning in early vaudeville's notion of "family entertainment." In 1907, impresario Florenz Ziegfeld introduced his first *Follies*, his American answer to the *Follies Bergère* of Paris, debuting a line of fifty beautiful chorus girls, stunningly clad, tapping in unison, putting an audible American stamp on a concept he adapted from the famous Tiller Girls of the London music halls, the first show dancers to dance in a precision chorus line.

These first revues were loosely organized, with no central theme, and they relied heavily on dance routines, comedy sketches, and musical num-

The original Ziegfeld Follies girls doing their famous tambourine and cane number.
The Bettmann Archive.

45

The first American chorus line: the Original Floradora Sextet, about 1900.
The Museum of Performing Arts, Dance Collection.

bers. In addition to the chorus lines, many individual introductions took place in Ziegfeld's revues, from the debuts of songstress Fanny Brice (1910) and dancer Ann Pennington (1913) to the first major appearances of comedians W. C. Fields (1915) and Will Rogers (1917). Other popular revues brought forth big names of their own. Ned Wayburn's *Passing Show of 1918* first starred the brother-sister team of young Fred and Adele Astaire. The entire score of George White's *Scandals of 1920* was written by a young composer named George Gershwin, and the first appearance of Bill Robinson on Broadway was in Lew Leslie's all-black revue, *The Blackbirds of 1928.*

The Rise of the Musical Comedy

George M. Cohan, one of vaudeville's flashiest figures and one of its most innovative hoofers as well, was also the father of America's special contribution to the world of theatrical entertainment: the musical comedy.

Famous among hoofers for his technique of dancing up the side of a wall and kicking his feet high over his head, Cohan gave the musical comedy form a distinctly American identity. For the first time, in *Little Johnny Jones* (1903), an evening of American musical entertainment was tied together with a distinct story line that linked the show's songs, dances, and humor with dramatic characterizations and themes, giving an overall unity to the performance.

Little Johnny Jones told the story of an American jockey who went to London to ride in the Derby and was falsely accused of conspiring with big-time gamblers to throw the race. This thin but workable plot was the perfect vehicle for Cohan's spectacular tap dancing and his bold chauvinism. Moreover, the show both dramatized and reinforced a growing national pride in things uniquely American—and Broadway took full advantage. Two classic numbers from *Little Johnny Jones,* "Give My Regards to Broadway" and "Yankee Doodle Boy," couldn't have come at a better time or in a better form for the development of the American stage. With Cohan's second musical, *Forty-five Minutes from Broadway* (1906), an even greater success, containing such immensely popular numbers as the title song and "Mary's a Grand Old Name," the fledgling art form was well on its way to popularity.

Broadway at this time was stocked with talented musicians and dramatists eager to participate in the development of the new form of theater. With men like Jerome Kern, Vincent Youmans, Sigmund Romberg, and the team of Richard Rodgers and Lorenz Hart, the era of musical comedy was off and running.

The last word in chorus lines: the Radio City Music Hall Rockettes, about 1950.
Jack Stanly.

Young George M. Cohan, the father of the American musical comedy.
New York Public Library at Lincoln Center, Theater Collection.

A show-stopping star on Broadway, Betty Bruce was one of the first women to use ballet technique in tap routines.
Bruno of Hollywood.

Tap Comes Together

The rise of the musical comedies and the success of both black and white revues on Broadway in the 1920s gradually brought about a fusion of tap influences that had been developed separately in the twin strains of white vaudeville and the T.O.B.A. circuit. One major figure in this common-law marriage was the black choreographer Buddy Bradley, who choreographed many of the revues and musicals of the twenties. In 1928, Bradley opened a studio on Broadway to teach the techniques of the black hoofers to the emerging group of young white musical performers. Among Bradley's students in the twenties and early thirties were Mae West, Ed Wynn, Eddie Foy, Clifton Webb, Ruby Keeler, Adele and Fred Astaire, Lucille Ball, and Paul Draper.

Bradley's instruction, however, was not just a one-way offering of black dance styles to white dancers. Bradley had derived much of his own technique from white jazz musicians like Frank Trumbauer and Bix Beiderbecke, and he preferred the music of white jazz soloists to that of black musicians. The white artists, he claimed, played with a drummerlike precision, hitting each note with a clarity that made their music easy to follow and enabled him to transform jazz instrumental solos into tap dance routines.

Baby Laurence, the great master of close-to-the-floor tap virtuosity, is pictured in an uncharacteristic balletic leap outside the Jazz Museum in New York City in 1972.
Jack Bradley.

49

Tap chorus in formation from Busby Berkley's *Gold Diggers of 1937.* Joan Blondell is in the foreground (Warner Brothers). *The Bettmann Archive.*

In the thirties and forties Betty Bruce was an outstanding tap dancer. She was something of a prodigy, making her debut at the age of six in the corps de ballet of the Metropolitan Opera. Her exciting dancing style evolved as she integrated the ballet technique into her tap routines. Miss Bruce made her mark on the Broadway scene stopping shows like *Something for the Boys* and *Up in Central Park.* Somehow, the greatly talented Betty Bruce never made the Hollywood musical scene, but it was Hollywood's loss.

Perhaps the most important arena for exchanges of tap styles during the twenties, thirties, and forties was the famous Hoofers Club on 131st Street and Seventh Avenue in Harlem. Here, in a downstairs back room at the Comedy Club, one of Harlem's better gambling establishments, tappers of all reputations and levels of expertise exchanged steps and held challenges in an informal but highly competitive atmosphere. Activities at the Hoofers Club were mostly among blacks, with greats like King Rastus Brown, John Bubbles, Bill Robinson, Bunny Briggs, and Baby Laurence taking on serious challengers and intimidating pretentious newcomers. But many professional white tappers made it uptown once a week or so to exchange steps and take part in generally good-natured competitions, as tap dancing beat out an integrated kingdom of its own. After generations of racism and ethnic rivalry, tap found its castle in Harlem, just up the road from the original melting pot.

CHAPTER FOUR

Hollywood and the Golden Age of Tap

Like tap dancing, the motion picture is a uniquely American creation, and the evolution of both tap and film from oddities into art forms is tightly linked in the history of American entertainment.

In the first "major" motion picture, Thomas Edison's 1903 version of *Uncle Tom's Cabin,* the inventor of the cinema preserved on celluloid an early version of the notorious Cakewalk. In a lively scene, the slaves in Harriet Beecher Stowe's Civil War melodrama perform a vigorous and animated plantation strut, which clearly depicts the original Cakewalk as a parody of the grand balls of Deep South society. The Cakewalk was not technically a "tap" dance, but major features of it were incorporated into later more percussive versions of minstrel and vaudeville dance.

But because tap dancing depends on sound, the silent film was poorly suited for capturing tap's audience appeal. From Edison's starting point, tap on film served only documentary purposes, and the pioneer days of Hollywood contributed nothing to the development of cinema tap dancing.

Then, Happy New Year, 1927! Sound came to film in Al Jolson's *The Jazz Singer,* and almost immediately film and dancing began a torrid romance that made American musical entertainment world-renowned for its vitality, spectacle, and humor. By 1929, one of the most chaotic years in the nation's and Hollywood's history, three out of four "talkies" featured dancing. With the innovation of the soundtrack, Hollywood stumbled on the sure-fire combination of image and music, and mammoth screen musicals began pouring out of Hollywood, each one trying to top its immediate

51

predecessor by staging the ultimate musical production number. Equipped with this new technology, filmmakers such as Busby Berkeley, Albertina Rasch, Sammy Lee, and Seymour Felix tried to outdo each other with grand-scale extravaganzas that took theatrical dancing far beyond the physical constraints of the Broadway stage.

The talking picture offered the opportunity for tap to develop beyond the simple entertainment purposes of vaudeville and stage revues. For starters, the first tap dance to music on film was not performed by an old-time hoofer but by an actress, Joan Crawford, in *Hollywood Revue* (1929). Dancing was not Crawford's forte, but she had apparently won a home-town Charleston contest in the mid-twenties, which gave her a leg up to Hollywood. Ironically, it was Joan Crawford who had the honor of being the first screen dancing partner of the man who single-footedly took tap dancing to its highest point of artistic achievement: the incomparable Fred Astaire.

Joan Crawford with choreographer Sammy Lee, rehearsing a dance for *Hollywood Revue of 1929* (MGM), the first talking film with tap dancing.
Museum of Modern Art/Film Stills Archive.

Within a few years of the advent of the talkie, the moviegoing public had viewed its fill of full-scale musical extravaganzas. By the time Astaire made his screen debut with Crawford in *Dancing Lady* (1933), the public was ready for a new approach to film dance. Astaire had one, and, from here on, the history of tap on film becomes a story of personalities.

The Men of Tap on Film

Fred Astaire

Born in Omaha, Nebraska, on May 10, 1900, Frederick Austerlitz became the man who gave tap dancing its image of stylish elegance. In his passage from awkward child star to debonair sophisticate in top hat and tails, Astaire accumulated years of experience as a vaudeville, ballroom, and ballet dancer, all leading up to his Hollywood years, when all his talents came together in an entirely new style of film dance, one that was perfectly suited to the developing movie musical comedy.

It wasn't until after Astaire showed up in Hollywood that anybody recognized his genius as a dancer. For over twenty-five years, he stayed in the background while audiences praised his older sister and earliest dancing partner, Adele. In 1906, when she was nine and he was six, the Astaire team was a major child act of vaudeville. Two years later Astaire entered an awkward stage, and the act lost its cuteness and fell apart for several years.

At this time, Astaire began ballet training, which enabled him eventually to expand his tap dancing style to include integrated movement of his entire body. This elementary ballet instruction was crucial to Astaire's development, since it taught him how to use other things than just his feet. Astaire's use of his arms, hands, and entire upper body was his monumentally important contribution to tap dancing, giving it a grace and dignity that it had never before enjoyed.

After years of training in tap, ballet, and ballroom dancing, Fred and Adele came back to the stage to star in Broadway musicals such as *Over the Top, Passing Show, Apple Blossoms,* and *The Band Wagon.* Fred was always considered the less spectacular member of the team, and it was not until 1925 that he worked out his first dance solo, in George Gershwin's *Lady Be Good.* Eventually, sister Adele married into high society and out of show business, and Astaire, on his own, was at last free to begin his great work.

In 1933, Astaire left Broadway for Hollywood. His first screen test was less than spectacular: "Can't sing. Can't act. Can dance a little." Undaunted, Astaire overcame his initial fear that the flat surface of the screen would rob dance of its three-dimensional quality and soon came to prefer film to the stage. There were no live audiences to contend with; he had the freedom to choose the best of several takes; and, above all, his

Fred Astaire and Joan
Crawford in Astaire's first
film, *Dancing Lady* (MGM,
1933).
New York Public Library.

Fred Astaire in action in the
forties.
MGM Publicity.

own "cool" style proved to have much more impact in cinema close-ups than under the proscenium arch.

Influenced by these strengths and preferences, Astaire, from the beginning, changed the entire nature of screen dance. He overturned the old notion that the happiest and most successful film dances were those that pretended to be part of some hyperbolic stage show. Instead, he introduced the idea that the best dances were those intimate, apparently impromptu numbers that sprang out of the action of the film's story.

In the same year of his debut with Joan Crawford, Astaire made his first film with the actress who is considered to have been his most perfect partner: Ginger Rogers. Together they starred in the classic *Flying Down to Rio* (1933) and went on to co-star in eight more films. With Ginger Rogers, Astaire raised tap dancing to new levels of sophistication. Under constant pressure to choreograph new dances, he blended traditional tap steps with ballet and ballroom technique, forming each dance into an artistic whole that was his trademark, innovation, and personal gift to the world of dance.

Fully integrated with the poise and nonchalance of Astaire's easygoing style was a firm sense of dramatic motivation. In fact, each Astaire number told a story of its own. It had a plot that was structured into a beginning, climax, and ending, with the primary purpose of entertaining, but with artistic form and style. Astaire's dances were directly related to the dramatic continuity of each film's story line, not just by chance, but in a conscious attempt to use the dance to advance or embellish the plot. In *Swing Time* (1936), for example, Astaire performs his famous Bojangles dance with three huge shadows of himself projected behind him on the scenery. In *Follow the Fleet* (1936), he does his famous dance along the deck to the music of the ship's great engines: In *A Damsel in Distress* (1937), Astaire dances around cars in the street, and in *Carefree* (1938), he makes his graceful way around the room, out onto the porch, then back into the room again.

Along with Bill Robinson, Astaire was one of the few dancers in the early musicals to make his own tap sounds on film. Because of the early complexities of uniting sight and sound, the first screen tap routines were kept relatively simple. As with the accompaniment in all musical films, tap sounds were meticulously worked out in studio rehearsal rooms and added to the films after the dancers had gone through their motions before the cameras. Even today, expert "dubbers" patch on the sound and coordinate it with the movement so that the whole screen performance seems real.

Eventually, Astaire's sharp clarity and masterful execution allowed him to film complex dance routines without any loss of authenticity. Confident of his ability, he took the dance steps themselves as a starting point for his higher cinematic aim, to integrate the dance into the story line, to make it a natural outgrowth of the developing plot. In *Theatre Arts Magazine* in 1973, Astaire explained his approach to film dance:

Fred and Adele Astaire with the chorus in the Broadway hit *The Band Wagon* (1931).
New York Public Library.

I think the audience always slumps—even more in movies than on stage—when they hear an obvious dance cue, and both the picture and the dance seem to lose some of their continuity. Each dance ought to spring somehow out of character or situation, otherwise, it is simply a vaudeville act.

A fan looks back:

> Fred Astaire was a salesman. He made it look so doggone easy. He made a truck driver feel like, "Gee, you can walk right into a dance"—until he got up and tried it himself and fell flat on his face. I have been in conflict with my fellow black hoofers, the board-beaters. They don't want to accept Fred Astaire because he's white. I wouldn't give a damn if he was a polka-dotted Chinaman: The guy's the greatest son-of-a-gun who ever tap danced, as far as I'm concerned. It's the truth.
>
> —**Alfredo Gustar**
> tap dancer in vaudeville and
> nightclubs; featured with Duke
> Ellington's band.
> New York, New York

The Musical Films of Fred Astaire

DANCING LADY (1933), with Joan Crawford
FLYING DOWN TO RIO (1933), with Ginger Rogers
THE GAY DIVORCEE (1934), with Ginger Rogers
ROBERTA (1935), with Ginger Rogers

Fred Astaire and Eleanor Powell rehearse a scene from *Broadway Melody of 1940*, the only film they made together (MGM). *Museum of Modern Art/Film Stills Archive.*

TOP HAT (1935), with Ginger Rogers
FOLLOW THE FLEET (1936), with Ginger Rogers
SWING TIME (1936), with Ginger Rogers
SHALL WE DANCE (1937), with Ginger Rogers
A DAMSEL IN DISTRESS (1937), with Joan Fontaine
CAREFREE (1938), with Ginger Rogers
THE STORY OF VERNON AND IRENE CASTLE (1939),
    with Ginger Rogers
BROADWAY MELODY OF 1940 (1940), with Eleanor Powell
SECOND CHORUS (1941), with Paulette Goddard
YOU'LL NEVER GET RICH (1941), with Rita Hayworth
HOLIDAY INN (1942), with Marjorie Reynolds
YOU WERE NEVER LOVELIER (1942), with Rita Hayworth
THE SKY'S THE LIMIT (1943), with Joan Leslie
YOLANDA AND THE THIEF (1945), with Lucille Bremer

Fred Astaire and Ginger Rogers together for the first time, in *Flying Down to Rio* (RKO, 1933).
Museum of Modern Art/Film Stills Archive.

ZIEGFELD FOLLIES (1946), with Judy Garland
BLUE SKIES (1946), with Joan Caulfield
EASTER PARADE (1948), with Judy Garland, Ann Miller
THE BARKLEYS OF BROADWAY (1949), with Ginger Rogers
THREE LITTLE WORDS (1950), with Vera-Ellen
LET'S DANCE (1950), with Betty Hutton
ROYAL WEDDING (1951), with Jane Powell
THE BELLE OF NEW YORK (1952), with Vera-Ellen
THE BAND WAGON (1953), with Cyd Charisse
DADDY LONG LEGS (1955), with Leslie Caron
FUNNY FACE (1957), with Audrey Hepburn
SILK STOCKINGS (1957), with Cyd Charisse
FINIAN'S RAINBOW (1968), with Petula Clark

Gene Kelly

After Fred Astaire, America's best known tap dancer is Gene Kelly. Born in 1912, Kelly started off in vaudeville with his family as the middle member of The Five Kellys and went on to become a lead dancer, actor, and choreographer. He first came to prominence on Broadway for his

The Five Kellys in an imitation of the famous Foys of vaudeville, about 1920. Gene, age eight, is in the middle. (*Left to right:* Joan, James, Gene, Louise, and Fred).
Fred Kelly.

60

Young Fred and Gene Kelly, 1930.
Fred Kelly.

lead role in *Pal Joey* (1940), one of the last musicals by the great team of Rodgers and Hart. Kelly then went to Hollywood and made his screen debut opposite Judy Garland as the "me" in *For Me and My Gal* (1942).

Kelly used his years in film to experiment with purely cinematic dance. He achieved special recognition for his famous "alter ego" dance in *Cover Girl* (1944), where he used trick camera work to produce a double image of himself in motion. In this film, Kelly used dance as a means of enhancing not just the story line but character as well, employing the alter ego technique to portray an inner conflict of the film's main character.

In 1952, Kelly starred in and co-directed *Singin' in the Rain*, perhaps the greatest musical film ever made. A hilarious story about the coming of the talkies, *Singin' in the Rain* was one of the first and most brilliant satires of the silent picture era. Kelly's joyous song and dance to the title number instantly became a film dance classic. In 1975, MGM re-released

Vera Ellen and Gene Kelly in On the Town (MGM, 1949).
Museum of Modern Art/Films Stills Archive.

the film, and a new generation of tap lovers flocked to see Kelly with his co-stars, Donald O'Connor and Debbie Reynolds.

Kelly was an outstanding cinematic personality. His strong arms and powerful physique gave him the look of a graceful athlete, and his energetic dancing seldom failed to evoke intense feeling and often sheer joy. In addition to his profound dance interpretations, Kelly emerged as an exceptional actor in his own right, appearing in several films in which he didn't dance at all, such as *The Black Hand* and *Marjorie Morningstar*.

Gene Kelly's classic song and dance in *Singin' in the Rain* (MGM, 1925).
New York Public Library.

The legendary Bill "Bojangles" Robinson.
New York Public Library.

The Musical Films of Gene Kelly

FOR ME AND MY GAL (1942)
DuBARRY WAS A LADY (1943)
THOUSANDS CHEER (1944)
COVER GIRL (1944)
CHRISTMAS HOLIDAY (1944)
ANCHORS AWEIGH (1945)
ZIEGFELD FOLLIES (1946)
LIVING IN A BIG WAY (1947)
THE PIRATE (1948)
WORDS AND MUSIC (1948)
TAKE ME OUT TO THE BALL GAME/EVERYBODY'S
    CHEERING (1949)
ON THE TOWN (1949)
SUMMER STOCK/IF YOU FEEL LIKE SINGING (1950)
AN AMERICAN IN PARIS (1951)
SINGIN' IN THE RAIN (1952)
BRIGADOON (1954)
DEEP IN MY HEART (1954)
IT'S ALWAYS FAIR WEATHER (1955)
INVITATION TO THE DANCE (1957)
LES GIRLS (1957)
LET'S MAKE LOVE (1960)
WHAT A WAY TO GO (1964)
LES DEMOISELLES DE ROCHEFORT/YOUNG GIRLS
    OF ROCHEFORT (1966)

Bill Robinson

Already mentioned in an earlier chapter, Mr. Bojangles must also be listed here with the major figures of tap's Golden Age. Best remembered on film for his dances with Shirley Temple in *The Little Colonel* and *The Littlest Rebel*, Robinson's easygoing dance style and gentle, fatherly image helped make him Hollywood's first black superstar. Already a legend in both black and white vaudeville before heading west in the early thirties, Robinson was in his late fifties when he started his film career.

The Musical Films of Bill Robinson

HOORAY FOR LOVE (1935)
BIG BROADCAST OF 1936 (1935)
THE LITTLE COLONEL (1935)
THE LITTLEST REBEL (1935)
DIMPLES (1936)
ONE MILE FROM HEAVEN (1937)

REBECCA OF SUNNYBROOK FARM (1938)
JUST AROUND THE CORNER (1938)
UP THE RIVER (1938)
STORMY WEATHER (1943)

In addition to tap's great three—Fred Astaire, Gene Kelly, and Bill Robinson—many other male tap stars made the transition from the stage to the screen. The following list includes the better known ones:

George Murphy

Murphy, a dancer and actor, went on to play his most believable role as U.S. senator from California. He first appeared on Broadway as a chorus boy and was eventually signed by Samuel Goldwyn for the film *Kid Millions* (1934).

The Musical Films of George Murphy

KID MILLIONS (1934)
AFTER THE DANCE (1935)
TOP OF THE TOWN (1937)
BROADWAY MELODY OF 1938 (1937)
YOU'RE A SWEETHEART (1937)
HOLD THAT CO-ED (1938)
LITTLE MISS BROADWAY (1938)
BROADWAY MELODY (1940)
LITTLE NELLY KELLY (1940)
TWO GIRLS ON BROADWAY (1940)
RINGSIDE MAISIE (1941)
RISE AND SHINE (1941)
LAS VEGAS NIGHTS/THE GAY CITY (1941)
MAYOR OF FORTY-FOURTH STREET (1942)
THE POWERS GIRL (1942)
FOR ME AND MY GAL (1942)
THIS IS THE ARMY (1943)
BROADWAY RHYTHM (1944)
SHOW BUSINESS (1944)
STEP LIVELY (1944)
BIG CITY (1948)

Dan Dailey

A tall, dapper leading man, Dailey first teamed up with Betty Grable in vaudeville and on Broadway. An MGM talent scout found him first, but he came back from the war to become a star at 20th Century-Fox.

George Murphy and Eleanor Powell in *Broadway Melody of 1940*.
Museum of Modern Art Film Stills Archive.

The Musical Films of Dan Dailey

HULLABALOO (1940)
ZIEGFELD GIRL (1941)
LADY BE GOOD (1941)
MOON OVER HER SHOULDER (1941)
PANAMA HATTIE (1942)
GIVE OUT, SISTERS (1942)
MOTHER WORE TIGHTS (1947)
WHEN MY BABY SMILES AT ME (1948)
YOU WERE MEANT FOR ME (1948)
GIVE MY REGARDS TO BROADWAY (1948)
YOU'RE MY EVERYTHING (1949)
A TICKET TO TOMAHAWK (1950)
I'LL GET BY (1950)
MY BLUE HEAVEN (1950)
CALL ME MISTER (1951)
MEET ME AT THE FAIR (1953)
THE GIRL NEXT DOOR (1953)

Fred Astaire, Eleanor Powell, and George Murphy in *Broadway Melody of 1940* (MGM).
New York Public Library.

Gene Kelly, Dan Dailey, and Michael Kidd doing a "Shuffle Off to Buffalo" in *It's Always Fair Weather* (MGM, 1955).
Museum of Modern Art/Film Stills Archive.

THERE'S NO BUSINESS LIKE SHOW BUSINESS (1954)
IT'S ALWAYS FAIR WEATHER (1955)
MEET ME IN LAS VEGAS/VIVA LAS VEGAS (1956)
THE BEST THINGS IN LIFE ARE FREE (1956)
PEPE (1960)

James Cagney

The little tough guy, Cagney danced in vaudeville and was acclaimed as a female impersonator before going on to Broadway and films in 1930. Few fans of his gangster films realize Cagney's solid background as a dancer. In 1942, he won an Academy Award for his outstanding portrayal of George M. Cohan in *Yankee Doodle Dandy*.

The Musical Films of James Cagney

BLONDE CRAZY (1931)
FOOTLIGHT PARADE (1933)
SOMETHING TO SING ABOUT (1937)
YANKEE DOODLE DANDY (1942)
WEST POINT STORY/FINE AND DANDY (1950)
STARLIFT (1951)
THE SEVEN LITTLE FOYS (1955)
LOVE ME OR LEAVE ME (1955)

Dapper Dan Dailey, with straw hat and cane, on the carnival stage in Irving Berlin's *There's No Business Like Show Business* (20th-Century Fox, 1954).
Museum of Modern Art/Film Stills Archive.

Donald O'Connor

One of those glowing child stars, O'Connor was born into vaudeville and played his first major film role as Bing Crosby's kid brother in *Sing You Sinners* (1938). He developed into a first-rate comedian as well as dancer, highly acclaimed for his clown number, "Make 'Em Laugh," in *Singin' in the Rain* (1952). O'Connor's film partners included Peggy Ryan, Debbie Reynolds, and Francis the Talking Mule.

The Musical Films of Donald O'Connor

MELODY FOR TWO (1937)
SING YOU SINNERS (1938)
ON YOUR TOES (1939)
WHAT'S COOKIN'? (1942)
PRIVATE BUCKAROO (1942)
GIVE OUT, SISTERS (1942)
GET HEP TO LOVE/SHE'S MY LOVELY (1942)
STRICTLY IN THE GROOVE (1942)

WHEN JOHNNY COMES MARCHING HOME (1942)
IT COMES UP LOVE (1943)
MR. BIG (1943)
TOP MAN (1943)
CHIP OFF THE OLD BLOCK (1944)
FOLLOW THE BOYS (1944)
THIS IS THE LIFE (1944)
THE MERRY MONAHANS (1944)
BOWERY TO BROADWAY (1944)
PATRICK THE GREAT (1945)
SOMETHING IN THE WIND (1947)
ARE YOU WITH IT? (1948)
FEUDIN' FUSSIN' AND A-FIGHTIN' (1948)
YES, SIR, THAT'S MY BABY (1949)

James Cagney's Oscar-winning portrayal of George M. Cohan in
Yankee Doodle Dandy (Warner Brothers, 1942).
Museum of Modern Art/Film Stills Archive.

Donald O'Connor in *I Love Melvin* (MGM, 1953).
Museum of Modern Art/Film Stills Archive.

CURTAIN CALL AT CACTUS CREEK/TAKE THE STAGE (1950)
THE MILKMAN (1950)
DOUBLE CROSSBONES (1951)
SINGIN' IN THE RAIN (1952)
I LOVE MELVIN (1953)
CALL ME MADAM (1953)
WALKIN' MY BABY BACK HOME (1953)
THERE'S NO BUSINESS LIKE SHOW BUSINESS (1954)
ANYTHING GOES (1956)

Ray Bolger

Rubber-limbed dancing comedian Ray Bolger is better known in theater than in film. Famous as the Scarecrow in *The Wizard of Oz,* Bolger's dancing reputation was enshrined on Broadway in *Where's Charley?* (1948), where he sang and laid down a show-stopping soft shoe to "Once in Love with Amy," a role he later re-created in the film version.

The Musical Films of Ray Bolger

THE GREAT ZIEGFELD (1936)
ROSALIE (1937)
SWEETHEARTS (1938)
THE WIZARD OF OZ (1939)
SUNNY (1941)
FOUR JACKS AND A JILL (1941)
STAGE DOOR CANTEEN (1943)
THE HARVEY GIRLS (1946)
LOOK FOR THE SILVER LINING (1949)
MAKE MINE LAUGHS (1949)
WHERE'S CHARLEY? (1952)
APRIL IN PARIS (1952)
BABES IN TOYLAND (1961)

The Nicholas Brothers

One of the great acrobatic tap teams of Hollywood, Fayard and Harold Nicholas had a meteoric rise from their initial success on a Philadelphia radio program, *The Horn and Hardart Kiddie Hour.* Soon after, they opened at the Cotton Club in Harlem, when Fayard was fourteen and Harold only eight. Before long, they had twisted, flipped, and tapped their way to Hollywood, where they first appeared with Eddie Cantor in *Kid Millions.* One of the leading "flash acts" of the thirties, they performed in Hollywood, on Broadway, on nightclub and concert tours, and extensively in Europe, Africa, and South America.

Ray Bolger re-creating his legendary soft shoe in the film version of *Where's Charley* (Warner Brothers, 1952). *Springer/Bettmann Film Archive.*

The Musical Films of the Nicholas Brothers

KID MILLIONS (1934)
BIG BROADCAST OF 1936 (1935)
DOWN ARGENTINE WAY (1940)
TIN PAN ALLEY (1940)
THE GREAT AMERICAN BROADCAST (1941)
SUN VALLEY SERENADE (1941)
ORCHESTRA WIVES (1942)
STORMY WEATHER (1943)
THE PIRATE (1948)

Johnny Coy

Born in 1924, Coy had a brief film career as a flippant young man who happened to be a skillful tap dancer as well. He danced on Broadway with Mary Martin before signing with Paramount.

The Musical Films of Johnny Coy

BRING ON THE GIRLS (1945)
THAT'S THE SPIRIT (1945)
ON STAGE EVERYBODY (1945)
DUFFY'S TAVERN (1945)
EARL CARROLL SKETCH BOOK/HATS OFF TO RHYTHM (1946)
LADIES' MAN (1947)
TOP BANANA (1954)

The Young Nicholas Brothers in the early thirties.
New York Public Library.

The Nicholas Brothers in *Down Argentina Way* (20th-Century Fox, 1940).
Museum of Modern Art/Film Stills Archive.

Gene Nelson

Nelson started off ice skating with Sonja Henie, then went on to tap dance on Broadway and become a leading musical comedy star for Warner Brothers. He had his first leading role in *Lullaby of Broadway* and co-starred with Doris Day in later musical hits.

The Musical Films of Gene Nelson

I WONDER WHO'S KISSING HER NOW (1947)
THE DAUGHTER OF ROSIE O'GRADY (1950)
TEA FOR TWO (1950)
WEST POINT STORY/FINE AND DANDY (1950)
LULLABY OF BROADWAY (1951)

PAINTING THE CLOUDS WITH SUNSHINE (1951)
STARLIFT (1951)
SHE'S WORKING HER WAY THROUGH COLLEGE (1952)
SHE'S BACK ON BROADWAY (1953)
THREE SAILORS AND A GIRL (1953)
SO THIS IS PARIS (1955)
OKLAHOMA! (1955)

Buddy Ebsen

Known worldwide as Uncle Jed of TV's *Beverly Hillbillies*, Ebsen started

Gene Nelson in his first starring film role, *Lullaby of Broadway* (Warner Brothers, 1951).
Museum of Modern Art/Film Stills Archive.

off as a soda jerk and later starred as an eccentric dancer, in vaudeville. In *Captain January*, he danced "At the Codfish Ball" with Shirley Temple.

The Musical Films of Buddy Ebsen

BROADWAY MELODY OF 1936 (1935)
BORN TO DANCE (1936)
BANJO ON MY KNEE (1936)
CAPTAIN JANUARY (1936)
BROADWAY MELODY OF 1938 (1937)
GIRL OF THE GOLDEN WEST (1938)
MY LUCKY STAR (1938)
THEY MET IN ARGENTINA (1941)
SING YOUR WORRIES AWAY (1942)
RED GARTERS (1954)
BREAKFAST AT TIFFANY'S (1961)
THE ONE AND ONLY GENUINE ORIGINAL FAMILY BAND (1967)

Judy Garland, age thirteen, with Buddy Ebsen in
Broadway Melody of 1938 (MGM).
Museum of Modern Art/Film Stills Archive.

The Women of Tap on Film

Ruby Keeler

It was Hollywood's wont to turn apple-cheeked hometown girls into glamorous movie queens, and in the thirties women at last came into their own as tap dancers. Among the first was Ruby Keeler, originally signed by Ziegfeld for *Whoopee* and later the star of the Broadway hit *No, No, Nanette* (1925). For a time the wife of jazz singer Al Jolson, Keeler made many movies, which transferred her stage tap talents to the screen.

As she readily admits, Keeler's footwork was nothing spectacular, but she knew her limitations and kept her dancing straightforward and clear. Trained in the style of the old hoofers, with very little body movement, Keeler didn't employ ballet turns or succumb to any of the more acrobatic fashions of Hollywood spectaculars. Throughout her career she remained a charming, innocent youth, but this made her very popular, and she developed a broad following.

From a technical standpoint, Ruby Keeler was no terror on the dance floor, but you had to like her. With her frequent partner Dick Powell, she seemed to dance like a man, although she remained at all times sweet and ladylike. In 1971, she made a great comeback on Broadway in the hit revival of *No, No, Nanette*, proving at sixty-two what a hoofing grandmother can do.

The Musical Films of Ruby Keeler

SHOW GIRL IN HOLLYWOOD (1930)
FORTY-SECOND STREET (1933)
FOOTLIGHT PARADE (1933)
GOLD DIGGERS OF 1933 (1933)
DAMES (1934)
FLIRTATION WALK (1934)
GO INTO YOUR DANCE (1935)
SHIPMATES FOREVER (1935)
COLLEEN (1936)
READY, WILLING AND ABLE (1937)
SWEETHEART OF THE CAMPUS (1941)

Eleanor Powell

A born performer with an athlete's body, Powell was perhaps the champion of women tappers in film. She started dancing at eleven and opened in a Miami nightclub at thirteen. Three years later, in 1928, she hit Broadway, where she developed her own distinctive heel and toe movements before going on to Hollywood in 1935.

Powell played opposite Fred Astaire in only one film, *Broadway Melody*

Al Jolson and Ruby Keeler,
who were also partners in
marriage. *New York Public
Library.*

of 1940, so she had many opportunities to carry the lead dance roles in her films. She tapped with intricate but very clear footwork, and her turns were executed with stunning beauty. Her body held a beautiful line—from the extension of her legs in very high kicks to the graceful movement of her arms. Like Astaire, Powell succeeded in combining balletic style with very fast tap footwork. She could hold her own with any of the best male tap technicians and was one of the few film tap dancers to do all her own choreography.

The Musical Films of Eleanor Powell

GEORGE WHITE'S SCANDALS OF 1935 (1935)
BROADWAY MELODY OF 1936 (1935)
BORN TO DANCE (1936)
BROADWAY MELODY OF 1938 (1937)
ROSALIE (1937)
HONOLULU (1939)
BROADWAY MELODY OF 1940 (1940)
LADY BE GOOD (1941)
SHIP AHOY (1942)

Ruby Keeler with the chorus line of *Forty-second Street* (Warner Brothers, 1933). *Museum of Modern Art/Film Stills Archive.*

Eleanor Powell shakes hands with famed drummer Buddy Rich after Tap and Drum challenge in *Ship Ahoy.*
Museum of Modern Art.

I DOOD IT/BY HOOK OR BY CROOK (1943)
THOUSANDS CHEER (1944)
SENSATIONS OF 1945 (1944)
THE DUCHESS OF IDAHO (1950)

Ann Miller

On stage at five, in George White's *Scandals* on Broadway at eighteen, Ann Miller was eventually spotted dancing in a Hollywood nightclub and promptly signed for the film *New Faces of 1937*. A stunning performer, she displayed fabulous footwork and flashy turns, but while she was always the featured dancer in her films, she was never given the opportunity to play top star. Finally, in 1969, she played the singing and dancing role of *Mame* on Broadway, proving once and for all her ability to carry the lead role in a musical.

The Musical Films of Ann Miller

NEW FACES OF 1937 (1937)
LIFE OF THE PARTY (1937)
RADIO CITY REVELS (1938)
TARNISHED ANGEL (1938)
HAVING A WONDERFUL TIME (1938)
IT'S THE DOCTOR'S ORDERS (1939)
HIT PARADE OF 1941 (1940)
TOO MANY GIRLS (1940)
MELODY RANCH (1940)
GO WEST, YOUNG LADY (1941)
TIME OUT FOR RHYTHM (1941)
PRIORITIES ON PARADE (1942)
TRUE TO THE ARMY (1942)
WHAT'S BUZZIN' COUSIN? (1943)
REVEILLE WITH BEVERLY (1943)
HEY, ROOKIE (1944)
JAM SESSION (1944)
CAROLINA BLUES (1944)
EADIE WAS A LADY (1945)
EVE KNEW HER APPLES (1945)
THRILL OF BRAZIL (1946)
EASTER PARADE (1948)
THE KISSING BANDIT (1949)
ON THE TOWN (1949)
TEXAS CARNIVAL (1951)
TWO TICKETS TO BROADWAY (1951)
LOVELY TO LOOK AT (1952)

Ann Miller in *Hit the Deck* (MGM, 1955).
New York Public Library.

SMALL TOWN GIRL (1953)
KISS ME KATE (1953)
DEEP IN MY HEART (1954)
HIT THE DECK (1955)
THE OPPOSITE SEX (1956)

Shirley Temple

The Model-T of child stars, Shirley Temple sang, tapped, and acted her way into the hearts of anyone who was ever a child. Born in 1928 with huge dimples to a persistent mother, her first major role, in *Stand Up and Cheer*, led to a contract with 20th Century-Fox, which brought her an Oscar at six for bringing "more happiness to millions of children and millions of grown-ups than any child of her years in the history of the world." She

Ann Miller in *Two Tickets to Broadway* (RKO, 1951).
Museum of Modern Art/Film Stills Archive.

first teamed up with dance instructor and leading man Bill Robinson in *The Little Colonel*, then both performed his famous Stair Dance in *The Littlest Rebel*. On her own, Shirley impersonated both Fred Astaire and Ginger Rogers in *Stowaway*.

The Musical Films of Shirley Temple

BOTTOMS UP (1934)
CAROLINA (1934)
STAND UP AND CHEER (1934)
CHANGE OF HEART (1934)
LITTLE MISS MARKER/GIRL IN PAWN (1934)
BABY TAKE A BOW (1934)
NOW AND FOREVER (1934)
BRIGHT EYES (1934)
THE LITTLE COLONEL (1935)
CURLY TOP (1935)
THE LITTLEST REBEL (1935)

Shirley Temple and Bill Robinson do their famous military tap number in *Rebecca of Sunnybrook Farm* (20th-Century Fox, 1938).

CAPTAIN JANUARY (1936)
POOR LITTLE RICH GIRL (1936)
DIMPLES (1936)
STOWAWAY (1936)
WEE WILLIE WINKIE (1937)
HEIDI (1937)
REBECCA OF SUNNYBROOK FARM (1938)
LITTLE MISS BROADWAY (1938)
JUST AROUND THE CORNER (1938)
THE LITTLE PRINCESS (1939)
THE BLUEBIRD (1940)
YOUNG PEOPLE (1940)
KATHLEEN (1941)
MISS ANNIE ROONEY (1942)

Vera-Ellen

Vera-Ellen started dancing at ten and became one of the most versatile dancers on film. Trained in tap, ballet, acrobatic, and dramatic dancing, she had been a Rockette and specialty dancer on Broadway before being signed by Samuel Goldwyn to make the film *Wonder Man* with Danny Kaye.

The Musical Films of Vera-Ellen

WONDER MAN (1945)
THE KID FROM BROOKLYN (1946)
THREE LITTLE GIRLS IN BLUE (1946)
CARNIVAL IN COSTA RICA (1947)
WORDS AND MUSIC (1948)
LOVE HAPPY (1949)
ON THE TOWN (1949)
THREE LITTLE WORDS (1950)
HAPPY GO LOVELY (1951)
BELLE OF NEW YORK (1952)
CALL ME MADAM (1953)
WHITE CHRISTMAS (1954)
LET'S BE HAPPY (1957)

Ginger Rogers

Astaire's first and best film dancing partner, Ginger Rogers was known not so much for her own dancing as for the way she complimented Astaire. Of all Astaire's dancing partners, her petite size and vivacious personality were the best. match for his urbane sophistication and lanky frame. Over and above her ebullient personality and flair, Rogers's dynamic acting ability was proven when she went on to win an Academy Award for her performance in *Kitty Foyle*.

Vera-Ellen in *White Christmas* (Paramount, 1954).
Museum of Modern Art/Film Stills Archive.

The Musical Films of Ginger Rogers

YOUNG MAN OF MANHATTAN (1930)
QUEEN HIGH (1930)
THE SAP FROM SYRACUSE (1930)
FOLLOW THE LEADER (1930)
CARNIVAL BOAT (1932)
HAT CHECK GIRL (1932)
FORTY-SECOND STREET (1933)
BROADWAY BAD (1933)
GOLD DIGGERS OF 1933 (1933)
SITTING PRETTY (1933)
FLYING DOWN TO RIO (1933)
TWENTY MILLION SWEETHEARTS (1934)
CHANGE OF HEART (1934)
THE GAY DIVORCEE (1934)
ROBERTA (1935)
TOP HAT (1935)
IN PERSON (1935)
FOLLOW THE FLEET (1936)
SWING TIME (1936)
SHALL WE DANCE? (1937)
HAVING A WONDERFUL TIME (1938)
VIVACIOUS LADY (1938)
CAREFREE (1938)
THE STORY OF VERNON AND IRENE CASTLE (1939)
TALES OF MANHATTAN (1942)
LADY IN THE DARK (1944)
WEEKEND AT THE WALDORF (1945)
THE BARKLEYS OF BROADWAY (1949)
THE FIRST TRAVELLING SALESLADY (1956)

Tapping to the Classics

In the Golden Age of Hollywood, American tap dancing reached an artistic peak. With innovative performers like Fred Astaire, Gene Kelly, and Eleanor Powell, tap reached new heights of complexity and refinement, yet always within the context of popular entertainment and at bottom remaining faithful to its early folk roots. From there, tap as a popular art form appeared to have little direction in which to grow during the forties.

A possible exception was in the area of concert performance, a field pioneered by Paul Draper. Born into a serious musical family, not really in his element on Broadway or in Hollywood, Draper made a conscious

Paul Draper, the great concert tap dance artist, in a stag leap, 1954.
Barrett Gallagher.

attempt to raise tap dancing to the level of a classical art. Instead of applying balletic technique to popular music, as did Astaire and Kelly, Draper adapted the principles of tap in a balletic style to classical music, attempting to demonstrate the versatility of the dance form and provide a new medium for its expression in the concert performance.

Throughout the forties, Draper and his partner, harmonica virtuoso Larry Adler, toured the nation to wide acclaim. Tapping to the music of Bach, Draper's feet would play a counterpoint to the score. Undaunted by convention, he would as easily tackle Scarlatti as Mozart. Unfortunately, as with a number of other entertainers of the period, Draper's career was dealt a fatal blow at its peak by the political pressures of the McCarthy era. Although performing rarely today, Draper, a brilliant innovator, continues to teach and pass on his masterful classical technique.

In response to Draper's efforts, composer Morton Gould wrote *Tap Dance Concerto*, the first composition ever created that made use of the sound of the dancer's feet as a solo instrument in a concerto with orchestra. The concerto is in four relatively short movements. The first is an animated "Toccata" with an extended solo cadenza near the end. This is followed by a slower, quietly subdued "Pantomime," a graceful "Minuet," and a brilliant, rapid-fire "Rondo."

In composing *Tap Dance Concerto,* Gould has said that he "utilized the tap dance medium as an integrated rhythmic and dynamic part of the orchestral texture," adding that the dance patterns notated in the score "may be elaborated upon by the individual tap dance soloist, it being important, however, to keep the basic rhythmic designs so that the work has an organized and formal consistency." *Tap Dance Concerto* was first performed in the early fifties by balletic tap exponent Danny Daniels. The only dancer performing Gould's work today is balletic tapper Michael Dominico, who has appeared with the New York Philharmonic, the Cleveland Symphony, and many of the nation's other major orchestras.

With support from classical artists such as Draper and Gould, tap dancing would appear to have been permanently set in the American cultural landscape. The fifties, however, brought a decline in its popularity, and in a few short years, tap dancing all but vanished from the American scene.

CHAPTER FIVE

ℒost in the Shuffle

Around the mid-thirties, even while tap dancing was nearing its highest point of artistic achievement and popular acclaim, tides of change in American entertainment broke the wave that tap had been riding. New forces gradually pushed it off the stage and snipped it out of films, so that by the fifties footwork for the sake of sound had ceased to be a desirable element of contemporary dance performance, and tap was officially "dead."

Of course, many professional dancers claim that tap dancing never died. Numerous performers and instructors of tap say they made decent livings from their art throughout the lean years of the fifties and sixties, and there are those who will argue that no true art form can ever really pass away. But by the mid-point of this century it had become clear that something awful had happened to the joyous art of tap dancing. Tap acts were out of fashion. Tap dancers were out of work. In dancing schools around the country, a few pre-schoolers still continued their basic training in tap for poise and coordination, but it was no more than a childhood aid, like training wheels or braces, a phase they entered naturally and then outgrew.

It's tempting to look for a single cause on which to pin the rap for the murder of tap. Every professional dancer has a simple reply to the question, What killed tap dancing? Ballet. *Oklahoma!* Jazz. *West Side Story*. Television. Rock and Roll. It's almost as if the decline of tap dancing is an unsuitable topic for serious analysis. In fact, it became a fashionable habit among many modern dancers to degrade tap dancing as inconsequential and simply dismiss all mention of its death with a facile response.

Michael Dominico, one of today's young tap personalities.

The death of tap can be pinned to all of the above responses, and more; but the complete story of the decline of tap dancing in America requires some thoughtful unraveling and deserves some honest consideration.

Tap dancing started to die on Broadway even before it reached its height in Hollywood. By the early thirties, vaudeville was on the wane, the revue form was giving way to the story musical, and directors began to suspect that tap dancing could no longer sustain a full evening's entertainment. Robert Benchley wrote in *The New Yorker,* May 16, 1931:

> Up until three or four years ago, I was the Peer of Tap-Dance-Enjoyers . . . it didn't seem as if I could get enough tap dancing. But I did. More than enough. With every revue and musical comedy offering a complicated tap routine every seven minutes throughout the program, and each dancer vying with the rest to upset the easy rhythm of the original dance form, tap dancing has lost its tang.

Tamara Giva, George Church, Ray Bolger, and Basil Galahoff perform the revolutionary ballet *Slaughter on Tenth Avenue* in the 1936 production of Rodgers and Hart's *On Your Toes*, with choreography by George Balanchine.
New York Public Library.

Oklahoma, 1943. The death of tap began on Broadway when choreographer Agnes De Mille introduced ballet to the Broadway musical in Rodgers and Hammerstein's record-breaking production. Pictured is Joan McCracken (left) and ensemble.

This statement was made, ironically, as tap was about to become a major influence in Hollywood—two years before Fred Astaire's first film. But Benchley's observation applied only to the stage and was quite accurate.

There were many immediate causes for the beginning of the theatergoing public's disaffection with tap: overexposure, sloppiness, and lack of originality on the part of the performers. For whatever reasons, audiences no longer found tap satisfying; and it became clear that if the musical comedy was to survive, choreographers would have to give the audiences something more than straight, old-time hoofing. So they introduced ballet.

Tap dancing on Broadway received its first major body blow in 1936, when the musical *On Your Toes* featured the premier popular ballet sequence for "Slaughter on Tenth Avenue," choreographed for the stage by world-famous ballet artist George Balanchine. Suddenly, the developing form of musical comedy had a new tool to work with, a highly sophisticated and versatile form with which to further the development of the plot and increase the impact of the story. Unlike tap, which was strictly a performer's vehicle, ballet seemed to provide some natural extension of the very pretense of the stage. Before anyone tried it, ballet seemed to be too gentle and tender a dance form for the rough and tumble American stage.

Pajama Game, 1954. When Bob Fosse brought jazz dancing to the musical comedy stage, it began a new trend in theatre dance. Pictured (from left to right) are Ken LeRoy, Neile Adams, and Frank Derbas in "Steam Heat."

A dance at the gym, from *West Side Story*, 1957. Modern jazz conquered Broadway once and for all in this smash hit with score by Leonard Bernstein, lyrics by Stephen Sondheim, and brilliant choreography by Jerome Robbins. Never before had any musical used dance so effectively as an integral part of the plot development.
Springer/Bettmann Film Archive.

But from the moment it was tested in *On Your Toes,* ballet and musical comedy seemed to be natural partners.

> The death of tap on Broadway happened as a rebellion. It had to do with the fact that tap had stopped growing. It had become the art of the hoofer, but by that time choreographers were no longer dealing with that form. The integration of the dance into the piece was more important, the total theater employment was more important. There was no place in the writing of those musicals, then, where the show could stop and the hoofers would appear and belt out their number.
>
> **—Murray Louis**

In 1943, the era's other great ballet choreographer, Agnes De Mille, worked a ballet dream sequence into *Oklahoma!*, the first musical by Rodgers and Hammerstein. With the smash success of *Oklahoma!*, tap dancing was all but declared a nonentity on Broadway. Performers in the major musicals that followed traded in their tap shoes for toe shoes, and with the appearance of ballet numbers in *Bloomer Girl* (1944), *Carousel* (1945), and *Brigadoon* (1947), the new dance style became established on

Broadway. Tap had been replaced as the ruling force in musical comedy dance.

At the time, many dancers strong in other forms but having weak or no tap technique were happy to see tap go. They viewed it as trivial and un-artistic, an eccentric or insignificant dance. According to one tap master, the thirties was a period of civil war within the world of popular dance. The battlefield was the Broadway stage, and the terms of the contest were winner take all.

> I think some of the choreographers had a complex, because in the early days, if you went to an audition and you were a ballet dancer, why, they threw you out. They didn't want any part of you, up until *Oklahoma!* Prior to that, there was no place for ballet in musical comedy, so this gave them a complex, and I think they felt that tap was a terrible menace to them. I've always found this antipathy toward tap among ballet dancers because—no question about it—there's no way ballet is going to hold up against good tap, as far as audience appeal is concerned. Ballet dancers were afraid of tap exponents because they would invariably get the job. The result was that the story musical came along, and when they brought in choreographers from ballet, they would say, "All right, we'll get even with you," and they wouldn't hire a tap dancer.
>
> **—Jack Stanly**

As the forties progressed, the complete eclipse of tap by ballet on Broad-way was eventually felt across the country. In the major nightclubs in the East, and later nationwide, booking agents began to turn away from tap acts in favor of the new ballet rage. *Adagio* teams who performed balletic lifts and turns were in great demand, and for the first time, tap dancers in singles and teams, both black and white, began to feel the pinch. Then a new style of dance made its appearance on Broadway, offering a new challenge tap was unable to meet. Enter modern jazz dance.

In 1954 the musical *Pajama Game* introduced the choreography of Bob Fosse to Broadway. The major dance number, "Steam Heat," performed by Carol Haney and featuring dancers Peter Gennaro and Buzz Miller, was an instant sensation. The modern jazz idiom had taken hold in the musical theater, appearing in an increasing number of shows, including *Damn Yankees* (1955), starring Gwen Verdon. Then, on September 26, 1957, at the Winter Garden Theatre, modern jazz conquered Broadway once and for all, as audiences went wild over *West Side Story*, the twentieth-century version of *Romeo and Juliet*, with Leonard Bernstein's masterful score, Stephen Sondheim's compelling lyrics, and Jerome Robbins's brilliantly conceived jazz choreography. Never before had any musical used dance so effectively as an integral part of the plot development. Moreover, the jazz feeling of *West Side Story*, expressed so vividly in both score and choreog-raphy, seemed especially appropriate as an expression of American life in the fifties.

> The first thing I learned to do when I was five years old . . . my first dancing lesson was a tap lesson. And then during the drought—the fifties and sixties—

bye, bye to tap. In fact, when I got to New York, I didn't even admit that I knew how to tap—that just meant you were from the sticks. It just wasn't being done here. All the rage was jazz dancing.

> **—Tommy Tune**
> Tony Award-winning tap dancing
> star of the Broadway musical
> *Seesaw*; Broadway, TV, and film
> dancer-choreographer
> New York, New York

Popular tastes had been gradually shifting since the thirties, as the developing electronic media brought forth an ever-increasing flow of words, sounds, and images, prompting more sophisticated responses from audiences. The quality of life was increasingly complex, requiring new artistic forms for its proper expression. Traditional tap simply couldn't keep up.

> Why did tap die out? I suspect largely because the other forms of dance which began to emerge in other shows were so much more imaginative, so much more musical, and so much more meaningful that nothing as ordinarily idly based as tap dancing had been could conceivably survive in the face of it. The dancing that went into *Oklahoma!*, *West Side Story*, *On the Town*, and the ballets was of so much more imagination, skill, energy, strength, love, humor, wit, rhythm, musicality, that there was no place for anything as sheerly lightweight—that's not quite the word, but I can't think of a better one at the moment—as tap. With all the other things that other dancing was, I don't see how tap survived even as long as it did.
> **—Paul Draper**

While these new dance forms were changing the face of Broadway, a similar transformation was taking place in Hollywood. Broadway's battles were being fought at the artistic level, however, while Hollywood's course was being determined more by matters of finance and technology.

In the thirties and forties, even into the early fifties, young musical performers, singers and dancers with star potential, were put under contract by MGM, RKO, and other major studios. The budding talent was then enrolled in training and development programs under the eyes of seasoned star-builders. In the boom years of prolific musical film production, stars like Fred Astaire, Ginger Rogers, Gene Kelly, Bill Robinson, Shirley Temple, Ann Miller, Donald O'Connor, Peggy Ryan, Betty Grable, Dan Dailey, Vera-Ellen, Ruby Keeler, Eleanor Powell, Gene Nelson, Ray Mac-Donald, and Johnny Coy went from one musical to another. Audiences flocked to see the latest vehicles as quickly as they could be produced and distributed.

In the fifties, however, various cultural changes—primarily the rise of television—altered the face and function of Hollywood, and the studios gradually stopped producing their lavish musicals. Even the lower-budgeted musicals the smaller studios had been turning out with such regularity were rapidly becoming obsolete.

Commercial television made deep inroads into American entertainment patterns, and the results were disastrously felt at the cinema box office.

Michelle Lee, Tommy Tune, John Gavin, and chorus rehearsing *Seesaw*.

Caught up in the novelty of inexpensive home entertainment, people took quickly to the notion of "family togetherness"; and American film producers soon realized that they would have to go elsewhere for their audiences.

The export market provided the financial adrenalin that Hollywood needed for its survival, but the makers of musicals gearing their products for European or Japanese audiences encountered an insurmountable obstacle when dubbing foreign voices over American musical productions.

Imagine a cool Fred Astaire number being sung by a Japanese dubber. Or a gutsy Gene Kelly tune being belted out in German. Voice dubbing could be fairly effective with a straight talking film, but it created major problems with a musical. If Bing Crosby or Kathryn Grayson were the stars, one wanted to hear them sing the songs. Moreover, in translation, lyrics tended to lose their impact and different singing rhythms conflicted, which made dubbing of musical films for foreign audiences all but impossible.

Faced with the pressure of shrinking domestic markets and expanding foreign ones, filmmakers had no choice but to move in the most expedient direction. In the late fifties, the great American movie musicals, which audiences had enjoyed for so long, became things of our past. The studios could no longer afford to keep musical performers under contract; and as a result, the grooming and training programs were terminated. Hollywood's

Max Jacobson (*left*) as Roy Samuels, with Edith Fleming and Mut Samuels in *Boy Meets Girl* (1938).

output of major musicals dropped from a previous annual high of nine or ten down to a saddening single musical every year or two.

And what about television? Couldn't television, with its fanatical desire for mass popular appeal, reach out a helping hand to America's faltering tap tradition? It seemed like a fitting opportunity for this remarkable new device to declare its loyalty with the masses and leave the higher artistic squabbles of the ballet dancers and the jazz purists to the insular world of the Broadway stage.

But television failed to halt tap dancing's exile into the cultural wilderness. From the beginning, TV producers set about developing new forms of entertainment—the variety show, the talk show, the comedy hour—all of which seemed appropriate for some lighthearted dance relief. But tap was not enlisted to fill the growing need. One insider from TV's early days explains why.

> They refer to me as the first choreographer in television. When I went into television there was no network; it was CBS local. Then in '48, we went network, across the country. I did the first musical show on television, *The Lannie Ross Show*. Then I directed *The Steve Allen Show*, around '51 or '52. I insisted on having a tap dancer or dance act on the show because each show ran over an hour. I used more tap dancers in six months' time when I directed *The Steve Allen Show* than have played in the entire history of the Palace Theater. Television should have been *the* medium for tap dancing, but what happened was the sound men came in and insisted that they had to have extra men put on the mikes to pick up the taps. Then the sound engineers came in and said, "Well, then we have to have an extra man to ride them." Finally, the directive came down from above. It said: *No more tap dancers will be used on any shows going over CBS local or network*. This was sent to every director, and the reason given was the union costs.
>
> **—Fred Kelly**
> tap dancer, choreographer, dance
> instructor; brother of Gene Kelly
> Oradell, New Jersey

Another, more aesthetic, objection may have lain in the nature of television itself, with its relatively small screen.

> Film really is the ideal medium for dance. In contrast to television, the large screen can readily show the facial expression as well as the line of the dancer. Because of its limitations, television is more restrictive choreographically . . .
> I'll never forget a performance I saw of Bill Robinson at the Coconut Grove in Hollywood. It was attended by a group of dancing teachers. Afterwards, Robinson said to me, "Did you notice, they were all watchin' my feet, but their eyes should have been on my face 'cause that's where I was sellin'."
>
> **—Gower Champion**
> famous film dancer who became a
> three-time Tony Award winner on
> Broadway; director-choreographer
> of *Carnival; Bye, Bye, Birdie;
> Hello Dolly!; Sugar;* director of
> *Irene*

Despite union problems that stemmed directly from its special nature as a dance with sound, its status as a popular art form might have won tap a new home on television. Individual tap acts would certainly have fit in with the early variety-show formats. But with the network executives casting the final blackball, tap dancing was out of the picture—on the tube and across the country.

I got back from the war in '46 and it took my heart out. I was with the William Morris office, they were handling me; but when I got back all the theaters were closing and I thought, Gee, I should get myself a job. I couldn't hang around working two weeks and laying off four because, you know, when you're married and you have responsibilities, you can't just look at fame anymore. You have to do something to survive. It was a little hard trying to get a job, but I was lucky. I became a baker and a cook, then a restaurant manager. Now I'm one of the best caterers around, but, you know, I always craved show business.

> —**Max Jacobson**
> former vaudeville dancer; half of
> the Samuels Brothers tap dance
> team
> Spring Valley, New York

CHAPTER SIX

Tap Comes Back

When tap died and I had to eat, I got into portraiture, and then into interior decorating, and then into architecture and, as a sideline hobby, I developed the science of astrology and casting horoscopes. During all this time I once in a while would pass by the 50th Street dives west of Broadway and see the Buck dancers just hanging out in there, waiting for somebody to buy them a drink or give them some money to buy dope. While they were throwing their lives away, I was studying these various sciences and making my living that way, so that when tap dancing began to come back, my body was in good shape. I hadn't destroyed it with drugs or liquor or any of those things.
—**Alfredo Gustar**

When tap dancing died, too many other things were going on in the entertainment world for anybody to even take note, let alone mourn its passing. On stage, ballet and jazz kept everybody busy. In Hollywood, there was the booming export market. And television was so novel in itself that the joy of a new technology and the promise of the ultimate advertising medium easily generated new channels for creative energy.

Amidst these innovations, there was no reason to get upset over the disappearance of a relatively minor feature of our cultural heritage. In the fifties, tap dancing had nothing in common with either the popular entertainment or the social dancing of the day. Professional tap dancers were no longer in demand on stage, in films, or along major nightclub circuits. Except for a few dancers who from the beginning managed to market their acts as nostalgia, most tap dancers had to expand into other forms of dance. The tappers became jazz and ballet dancers, and tap teachers had to offer a variety of classes to keep their studios in business. For aspiring dancers, tap was relegated to an eccentric role within their broader dance repertoires. From a professional standpoint, the choreographic innovations

Honi Coles and Cholly Atkins performing Bill Robinson's famous
"scoot" step at the United Nations.
Jack Bradley.

of the forties and fifties made tap an instant relic, the black sheep of the
dance world, the poor relation of the family of dance.

In the early sixties, it first occurred to certain members of the jazz world
that a part of its own ancestry had vanished from the land. In 1963, jazz
scholar Marshall Stearns brought a group of the most famous black tap
dancers to the Newport Jazz Festival to demonstrate this neglected tradition of American popular art that was in danger of dying out forever. The
Newport audience saw performances by some of the few legendary tap
figures still alive at that time. Charles "Honi" Coles, Chuck Green, Peter
Nugent, and Baby Laurence showed their individual classic tap styles to
the jazz buffs of the day. Everyone there got the point Stearns was making:
These old men were the sole carriers of an art form whose technique was
bound to die with them. Where were the young dancers who would take
up the tap line where they left off? No one was even bothering to preserve
in some manner the unique contributions each of these men had made to
tap dancing. There was a sadness in that Newport performance, and an
implicit challenge.

104

A former dancer, Leticia Jay, felt the impact of Stearns's tap presentation and read the challenge as well. It took nearly six years to bring her project to fruition, but she finally assembled a troupe of the best remaining black tappers in an attempt to bring the almost forgotten art of tap to the attention of the art world and the larger public.

On March 16, 1969, Leticia Jay sent out mimeographed letters to leading dance figures in New York announcing her *Tap Happening* on the four Mondays in April at the Bert Wheeler Theater in the Hotel Dixie on West 43rd Street off Broadway. She invited everyone to participate in a second-half tap challenge, a traditional ad lib tap jam session in which all comers could show their steps and vie for stature with the assembled group of masters.

The troupe was enlarged during rehearsals by the challenge method used in the old Hoofers Club, the principle of challenge being a tradition dating back to Juba, John Diamond—all the way to the mills of Lancashire. From among the competition, they selected one white performer, Jerry Ames, to join the all-black company.

When *Tap Happening* opened, the cast included a rich mixture of tap talent ranging from the smooth, gentlemanly dance style of Chuck Green to the humorous lightness of big Rhythm Red, from Sandman Sims's unique performance on sand to Ames's ballet-influenced virtuoso style. The entire cast of *Tap Happening*—Jerry Ames, Lon Chaney, Chuck Green, Raymond Kaalund, Rhythm Red, Sandman Sims, Jimmy Slyde, Tony White, and Derby Wilson—gave New York audiences an evening of tap dancing that presented a living history of the form in a performance that communicated the excitement and importance of this re-emergence of tap on the New York stage.

The reaction surprised everyone. After years of apparent public indifference to the fate of tap dancing and tap dancers, the performers would have been satisfied if the response had been merely polite. Instead, *Tap Happening* enjoyed packed houses and rave reviews. The following weeks' audiences were widely heterogeneous; all ages and interests flocked to the theater, and *Tap Happening* became the dance event of the season.

By popular demand, *Tap Happening* was held over for eight more Monday nights. Whenever the performers heard that someone special was out front, they would try to coax him or her onstage to do a couple of freewheeling steps after the second-half challenge. Often people would oblige and jump onstage, tapping away with unrestrained abandon. Then the cast could call up anyone else who felt the spirit. After this participatory finale, other members of the audience would run up to the stage and vigorously shake the performers' hands, ask for autographs, and steal unabashed kisses.

Clearly, *Tap Happening* touched something in people, and after one performance producer Roger Euster came backstage with a proposal for the cast. He and Leticia Jay offered to co-produce an expanded production

Sandman Sims *sans* sand.
Boris Bakchy.

Jerry Ames rises to the challenge in The Hoofers' 1969 Broadway run. At left is Chuck Green, partly obscured Mabelee, and at right Rhythm Red.

with members of the same cast. *The Hoofers* opened for a regular run of eight performances per week at the Mercury Theater on July 29, 1969.

At last the dancers had a theater equal to their art. Microphones were placed underneath the fine wooden stage to catch every tap sound. The Tiny Grimes Jazz Band was well prepped for accompanying the tappers, and a blazing spotlight was supplied to add a sense of spectacle to the funky air. After tap dancing had been dormant for so long, the exultant

107

feelings of the dancers themselves poured over the footlights and infected the receptive audience. Initial responses of awe and reverence were soon overcome by jumping and shouting with joy.

The combined impact of *Tap Happening* and *The Hoofers* was profound. Critical approval was unanimous.

These performances have understandably become the talk of the dance world, and anyone interested in dance should on no account miss them.

—Clive Barnes
The New York Times

The dance form may be in for a lively revival . . . Whoever said that tap was limited in expression?

—Anna Kisselgoff
The New York Times

If tap dancing ever makes a comeback, old pros will say the road back started at the Bert Wheeler Theater. . . . The best thing about the program . . . is the ability of the hoofers to share their enthusiasm with the audience, something that seems rare in performances of any kind these days.

—Tom Tolnay
Backstage

Art? Well, of course. Beats all the requirements, including the rather rigid ones of my highbrow friend George Dorris, the dance critic and historian, who was sitting next to me. He said, "Sandman Sims gave the best dance performance I've seen since Eric Bruhn did his slow pirouette."

—Patrick O'Connor
The Jersey Journal

Tap dancing is the art of walking raised to a baroque magnificence. . . .

—Don McDonagh
The New York Times

To see the show is to realize it IS an art. . . . I was surprised by the amazing number of variations it is possible to incorporate into tap dancing.

—Alvin Klein
WNYC Radio

Tap Happening and *The Hoofers* put tap dancing back in both the public eye and ear, not simply as another blast in the nostalgia boom, but as a legitimate art form, a respected component of American dance and culture. Above all, tap came across as a rediscovered musical option and a stage possibility of proven audience appeal.

The next steps in the tap revival were not so much direct responses to the success of *The Hoofers* as they were natural outgrowths of attitudes that were beginning to take hold around the country. With the close of that burst of wild creativity known as The Sixties, unbridled Aquarian jubilation gave way to more thoughtful expressions of human energy than were previously tapped, and a general desire for a return to greater discipline and structure in activity. In addition, a new-found social awareness seemed to restore in people the impulse to confront their heritage without destroying it. These post-revolutionary attitudes proved receptive to the nascent revival of tap dancing.

Cautiously, without fanfare, tap dancing returned to Broadway. In the early seventies, tap routines were choreographed in traditional styles for major productions of old shows, such as *Dames at Sea,* and worked into modern versions of old-time Broadway, such as *George M.* Then in January, 1971, sixty-two-year-old Ruby Keeler brought her traditional hoofing style back to Broadway in a revival of the 1925 smash musical *No, No, Nanette.* Months of packed houses indicated that tap dancing was back, and its appeal was as strong as ever.

> When I first met Ruby Keeler, she said, "I just want you to know that I dance like a man because all my teachers were men tap dancers. In my day you went and learned routines. You went to a studio where other tap dancers were, where you exchanged steps and you made up routines. But I'm what you call a hoofer because I work close to the ground. I never had ballet, so I don't dance pretty like Eleanor Powell or Ann Miller." I was delighted to choreograph *No, No, Nanette* because I've always loved that particular genre of American theater dancing. I think we must never lose it, because it says what we are as much as, say, corn bread. And I wanted to show that all my early tap dance lessons weren't in vain.
>
> **—Don Saddler**
> Tony Award-winning choreographer
> who staged the revival of *No, No, Nanette*
> New York, New York

With *George M, Dames at Sea,* and *No, No, Nanette,* tap dancing regained a foothold on the Broadway stage. Suddenly, aspiring performers were asked to do tap numbers at auditions. For the first time in decades, tap dancing became a required component of any professional dancer's repertoire, and dance studios were flooded with breathless requests for emergency tap instruction.

> Well, it was actually when I came back to this country . . . when I came back from England, where I made *The Boy Friend,* which, happily, was all tap, that I decided to tap again. You know, making *The Boy Friend* really re-awakened me to tap. And I said, "What am I doing out on the Coast making television shows?" There were nine years of television as a choreographer and they were wasted. I really became stale, because nobody really wanted to know.
>
> I was making money, I had my own car, and I had a decent house on the Hill, but I wasn't happy. I had everything else that anyone had and I thought, well, this is it. But it wasn't it. It took my going over to England to make that film for me to realize what I was here for. I missed out on what I was here to do. So after I came back to this country, I came to New York, and I was only back for one week when Michael Bennett called. He said that he was in Detroit, that he was taking over a new show called *Seesaw.* That he had a tap number in it that needed to be done—reshaped—choreographed. Well, I did that and then I did another number, and finally I ended up in the show. I loved every minute of it.
>
> **—Tommy Tune**

In Hollywood, the movie moguls took their cue. In the spring of 1974, Metro-Goldwyn-Mayer released *That's Entertainment,* a full-length feature film that spanned Hollywood's Golden Era, the years from about 1925 to

1950. *That's Entertainment* presented for the first time in 70mm projection and wrap-around stereophonic sound the choicest scenes from nearly one hundred films produced at MGM when the studio's dictum was, "Do it big, do it right, and give it class." As a bonus, it blended newly filmed accounts of the personal memories of eleven of the stars who were at MGM during those years, including Fred Astaire, Gene Kelly, Donald O'Connor, and Debbie Reynolds. Among the classic films excerpted were *Anchors Aweigh, The Band Wagon, Born to Dance, Broadway Melodies of 1929, 1938,* and *1940, Dancing Lady, Meet Me in St. Louis, Rosalie, Singin' in the Rain, Words and Music,* and *Ziegfeld Follies.*

MGM's ambitious presentation was an overwhelming box office smash, and studio executives released a sequel in the spring of 1976. With the appearance of *That's Entertainment,* the glory that was tap dancing was once again put before the nation, and audiences applauded enthusiastically at the finish of each dance routine as if they were attending a live show. At last young people who had heard about tap dancing could see for themselves what everybody was talking about. The grace, elegance, cool, and above all, *fun* of tap dancing were clearly reflected on the screen. Once again, people experienced the outright pleasure of tap and many, set free by a decade of energy and activism, tried it for themselves.

Dawn Crafton's award-winning tap group, Performing Arts Competition, at the Dance Educators of America convention, 1975.
Jack Kerns.

In 1975, MGM's highly successful *That's Entertainment* contributed to a revival of interest in tap. Here Donald O'Connor and Gene Kelly dance in *Singin' in the Rain,* one of Hollywood's most popular musicals.
Museum of Modern Art/Film Stills Archive.

Tap dancing has something no other dance form has; that is, you have the ability to make your feet sing. And you can make that music with just your feet. Most jazz and ballet dancing has to do with your torso, your arms, your legs, your hips, your knees, your pelvic area, your whole attitude. But tap dancing is joy that really emanates from your toes and heels, nothing else. Now, if you add the rest of your body, then of course you have another dimension, but you are really singing from the lowest extremities up, and audiences love it.

But I think, to be really honest about it, tap will never be the number-one dance form in America again, either on stage or in films or on television. It will never be. Shows like *West Side Story*, which so successfully integrated dance to further the plot, changed the whole picture. I don't think that two people walking down the street in 1976 on a musical stage would stop to sing a song and then just by chance happen to have metal things on the bottom of their feet. You see, I think we've gone into reality a little bit too much for that.

But I feel that because of our continuing love of tap dancing, it will always be used at certain times by all the mediums. If you do a musical or a number with the feeling of the twenties, thirties, or forties, you put the taps on because that was the definitive dance form. And so today most professional dancers are aware that they must know tap along with their jazz and ballet. I believe it's a very important part of dance education. I would think that dancers now would be cutting down on the prospect of a lot of job opportunities if they don't have tap training.

So what I think has been proven, which is very heartwarming and very encouraging, is that tap will never ever die. Ever. There will always be that spot, where if you want an audience-grabber, a show-stopper, put on the tap shoes and make your feet sing.

—**Ron Field**
Tony Award-winning choreographer
of *Applause* and *Cabaret*
Los Angeles, California

As dance studios around the country began to fill up with amateurs, it became apparent that *That's Entertainment* had successfully scattered the seeds of a tap revival. Regardless of whether or not people were wholly mistaken, they began to view tap as an amateur activity. The great dancers made it look so easy, why not give it a shot? Here, in highly irregular procedure, ordinary people adopted for themselves a *performer's* dance.

Everybody says tap dancing has been dead. It's not. Tap dancing hasn't been dead, it's just that the people doing it haven't been doing it. It lost its art when rock and roll came out with all the noise and you couldn't hear the taps, but we didn't stop doing tap dances. We just kept it going right on. Now that it's come back, everybody says, "Oh, it's coming back. It's new!" It's not new; it's just an art that's been out there all the time.
—**Sandman Sims**

CHAPTER SEVEN

Tap's Next Steps

Now let me tell you this story. At a bar down in the Village, I met a girl
who is nineteen years old, who came from the Midwest. She has a perky,
sweet round face. She grew up on Shirley Temple movies and she said she came
to New York to become a tap dancing star. When I heard that, my eyes glazed
over. There was no humor there, no edge of New York sophistication. She came
from someplace in the Midwest to be a tap dancing star, and I didn't say
anything because the girl is really off in some fantasy. I could have pointed
out to her that nobody has become a tap dancing star since 1932, but I was
terrified by her. She's not being campy or funny or cute. She is dead serious,
and when I heard her, I thought, uh-oh, this little fad has gone too far.

—Patrick O'Connor

Will vernacular dance survive, and if so, how? Perhaps it disappeared only
to be reborn, transformed into something at present too fresh and strange. The
most highly developed dancing of the past—tap dance—is the most completely
lost, partly because it is so difficult, but also because a revolution in mass
culture apparently needs to begin all over again with something new and
relatively simple. . . . There is little reason to believe that the great tradition
of American vernacular dance has vanished forever, and much evidence to
support the belief that a new and perhaps more remarkable age of highly
rhythmic native dance will arrive in the not too distant future. Not the least
of our problems is to recognize it when it appears.

—Marshall Stearns
Jazz Dance, 1968

At this moment in our culture, tap dancing seems to be still poised on the
turning point it reached with the beginning of its revival in the late sixties.
Tap dancing is back, but the nature of its reincarnation is a matter for
speculation. Can tap in fact attain a respectful place among contemporary
popular art forms? Or is the recent revival merely a brief cresting of a

113

wave of nostalgia? Many important and concerned voices in the tap world express doubt and dismay at the manner in which tap has returned to American art and entertainment.

> Right now, in the old shows they're dancing it the same way we used to do it many years ago. It's fun to look at nostalgia, but it doesn't take you any further ahead into the future.
>
> **—Georgie Tapps**
> tap dancer in vaudeville,
> nightclubs, television
> Los Angeles, California

In fact, most of the tap dancing you see on stage today was developed and perfected thirty, forty, even fifty years ago. The steps are based on inventions of the 1800s, and the routines are copied from the great innovators of vaudeville days and Hollywood's Golden Era. In the tapping that is currently presented to the public, nothing new has been added in more than a generation. The course of the art form has been downhill since the heydays of Fred Astaire and Eleanor Powell. A dance instructor cites some reasons for tap's appalling stagnation:

> People are not making an attempt to be different. Everyone is watching television and trying to ape what they see on television. In the old days, God forbid you danced like somebody else! You wanted to be an individual, otherwise you were dead. Another problem today is that none of the girls wants to do comedy dancing. They don't want to be funny, they want to be pretty, they want to be sexy. And yet the greatest women in the theater were not pretty and they weren't sexy. They were funny. Fanny Brice and Sophie Tucker were not by the farthest stretch of the imagination *pretty*. They were funny, yes, but they weren't elegant. . . . Many people are going overboard with tap, and they're going to kill it—like they do so many things in our country—by overexposure. Because it's been neglected for so many years, tap dancing, both technique-wise and entertainment-wise, is not up to the caliber that it should be for this tremendous exposure, and that is worrisome. People need to be educated again. Like everything else we do in this country, we wait until the last minute or too late to do things we should have thought about yesterday.
>
> **—Jack Stanly**

There is a distinct possibility that tap as we have brought it back will fail us. In its old form it may not be strong enough to survive its own rebirth. If this happens, it will not be so much because the form lacked appeal but, as Jack Stanly states, because the performers lack the training to give tap a presentation that does justice to its beauty. If a weak and sloppy tap bills itself as the new state of the art, then the skeptics will move in for the kill. The ballet and jazz purists can wage the same assaults that accompanied their own flowerings in the forties and fifties. Once the form becomes confused with the performance, tap will sink back into the oblivion from which it so valiantly struggled to emerge. Then this often-expressed attitude may win out.

> Tap will forever be a nostalgia thing. It's an art that couldn't go anywhere. Draper was the end of the line. For one thing, you need an artist who would be as good as the greatest ballet dancer to take an art seriously that nobody takes seriously anymore. Ballet is serious because it is based on the myths of Western culture: the beautiful, unattainable woman, the heroic prince, the rape of the peasant girl. The themes of ballet have always been Western myths, but tap is sort of just there on its own.
>
> **—Patrick O'Connor**

The final challenge, then, is for tap to move out of the shadow of its nostalgic associations. It must go someplace other than where it has been in the past. But tap is in such a tenuous place artistically at the moment because no one has succeeded in moving beyond the old-time tap which, even without updating, has proved to be such a sturdy form of entertainment.

> Now that it's back on the boards again, I'm hoping that enough people will be interested in it and inspired to bring it ahead, to make it something along with ballet and modern dance. It can move ahead if the people that are portraying it are interested in improving what they're showing so that it's up to the level of sophistication that today's audiences require. Now they're accepting this thirty-year-old version with great relish, but imagine what it would be if the people got something superior to what they were doing thirty or forty years ago. What worries me today is that I haven't seen anything at dance conventions that gives me the impression that any effort is being made to improve the visual and the sound aspect of what tap should mean. They're still using the same movements, the same steps, which today are so corny. In other words, they're not making an attempt to utilize the training they've had in other fields, to put it along with what they've had from the past and make something a little bit more intelligent and entertaining out of it.
>
> **—Jack Stanly**

In the early thirties, when tap first started to wane in audience appeal, a generation of tap dancers came along who were ready and able to take the art form ahead, to hitch it to the rising star of ballet and create a more sophisticated, intricate art form. The merging of the two dance forms created a new style, an improved form of popular dance that brought together the joy and exuberance of tap and the grace and elegance of ballet. The question now is whether a new marriage of dance styles can take place.

> None of the arts are really overlapping. Ballet dancers are lousy folk dancers and rock dancers. Each skill is so specific that you spend your entire career mastering one. All basically employ the need to move, but what draws dancers to their professions are very strange things. With ballet dancers, there is a certain musical emotionalism, the spectacle, the corny, dreadful plots. This really grabs certain kids, and they want to immerse themselves in the nineteenth century. The thing that brings contemporary people to their art is their aversion to those things and the feeling for a more immediate sense of participation in the present. What brings tap dancers to their dance is a feeling

Hal Leroy, famed "eccentric" tap dancer, in *Harold Teen* (Warner Brothers, 1934).

for a certain style and no concern for other things, just that certain style. And, frankly, they like to pound the floor. They like the noise.

—**Murray Louis**

Dance forms have been combined, though, despite the varying motivations of their enthusiasts. Stearns points out that ballet and tap first came together years ago, even though the fluid spine and flexed knees required in tap dancing wreck correct ballet posture, just as pointing the feet at 45-degree angles in ballet make it extremely difficult to produce the tap sounds. Nevertheless, blending tap rhythms and ballet technique has proved possible. The task now facing dancers is to continue to expand this two-dimensional merger by working in more recent developments from jazz, rock, and other forms of modern dance. Once this is seen as desirable, it is up to the dancers to determine what form this new tap dancing will take.

I don't know what form it could take. I don't know what form anything might take. That's like asking, when Schönberg and Stravinsky were starting to write music, how will they write music? We don't know before it happens.

—**Paul Draper**

Indeed. We won't know in what new form tap will appear until it happens, but it is worth considering where this new form might come from.

Tap will always be there and available as a medium for choreographers. They're what's going to bring it back. If there is no need for it or use made of it in production, it's never going to come back. A conceptual person, in the beginning, will have to bring it back.

—**Murray Louis**

A sense of appropriateness may be important, as another famous tapper explains.

You can't just put a tap number in any show and say, well, here we'll do a tap number. If the show doesn't lend itself to a tap number, it's impossible to do it. It will stick out like a sore thumb.

—**Hal Leroy**
tap dancer in vaudeville, films,
television
Maywood, New Jersey

Tap dancing could take its great leap forward on Broadway, but the move would require a proper setting. A dance critic elaborates:

You have to go with your audience. If your audience is expecting nostalgia, you can't come on with a completely brand new development. But if you have a sustained audience that will go and see things and be receptive, then you can have the new developments, the progressive work. Yes, all it would take would be one choreographer. If Bob Fosse decided he wanted to put tap into a show, it would happen, but that's a creative decision. Look, it took Agnes De Mille—one person—to put the obligatory dream sequence in every Broadway show for twenty-five years. So one talented choreographer who wanted to do it and who respected the form could do it. Then I would think the critic would simply respond to what is presented on stage and say, I like it, or I don't like it.

—**Don McDonagh**
dance critic, *The New York Times*
New York, New York

That's all it would take. Perhaps one talented choreographer could spark a truly contemporary tap revival, but through the early seventies few people believed such a renaissance could occur on Broadway. In those years, the major hits did not come out of Broadway but *to* it. In drama, major successes were imports from the British stage. America's own musical hits were straight revivals such as *No, No, Nanette;* products derived from other eras such as *Grease,* a recreation of the fifties rock scene; and reverse adaptations such as *The Wiz,* which turned the classic film *The Wizard of Oz* into a lively, timely stage production.

In the mid-seventies, however, a vibrant new creativity came to Broadway. The stunning success of Michael Bennett's spectacular *A Chorus Line* raised interest in dance and dancers to an all-time high and gave Broadway a fresh awareness of its own role in American culture. The new-found pride spilled across the footlights; along with the producers and performers, critics and casual theatergoers alike opened up to experimentation, offering receptive praise to ambitious efforts such as *Pacific Overtures,* a daring, difficult attempt to work Oriental dramatic forms into an evening of Western entertainment.

In the mid-seventies, after a period of drifting, Broadway is once again alive with energy and ideas. In this dance-conscious era, amidst openness and enthusiasm, the new spirit of innovation could well lend itself to the development of a true seventies tap dance.

But how do you make a seventies tap dance? Amidst the dazzle and hoopla, it may be that Broadway is unable to provide the focus needed for earnest development of the art form.

How do you make a seventies tap dance? You cannot put it in a Broadway show because a Broadway show is expressing itself in other terms. I don't know if you can update it until somebody choreographs a terrific tap ballet, and then it will always be there for whenever it's needed. I should think that if there was a tap company formed that was brilliantly choreographed, the tap expression could work for that, but the expression would be in its own milieu. A tap company could use contemporary music, classical music, or anything. It's just sound—sound and movement. But you have to make sure that you're enhancing, via the sound and the movement, something that is dance-worthy. Then it doesn't need a period. You wouldn't have to know what year it was choreographed. If you want to ask, "How do we do a seventies tap?" then the subject matter has to be seventies, the music has to be seventies, and the expression of energy has to be a seventies society expression of energy.

—**Joe Layton**
Tony Award-winning choreographer
who staged *George M* on Broadway
Los Angeles, California

George Church, 1940. A strong balletic tap dancer of extraordinary technique.
James Kriegsmann.

Perhaps tap dancing has gone beyond Broadway, in which case a new form of tap may develop somewhere other than in musical comedy, possibly in a dance company. As we look to the wings for new possibilities, there is one further notion to consider. America's long-lost dance may have even gone beyond America.

I see it in Europe. I've been over there the last two or three years, teaching and doing concerts. Everybody there wants to tap dance. They see it as an American product, just like they look at jazz as an American cultural thing.

119

Jerry Ames.
Jack Mitchell.

They love it. They want to see more and more of it. They want to learn it. They want to do it because they really identify with American art and culture. They know enough about the classical ballet—you can't get any more elegant than that—but tap has a sort of individual creativeness about it, and I think they look at that as not so staid and stiff. Everybody has his own personal flair. The Europeans want to make up for the lack of respect that has been shown here. They want to make sure that tap dancing finds its proper niche in history. They appreciate it because they take the time to. Here, we've seen everything, we've done everything, and we put no importance on anything. We had our chance and we blew it. Now the Europeans are taking over. I think that's where your next great tap dancer is going to come from, Europe—either Switzerland or France. I really believe that, because folk dancing is a very important part of their lives. I've run across two or three people that you're really going to hear from. No name-dropping now, but remember I said it.

—**Jimmy Slyde**
tap dancer; featured in *Tap Happening* and *The Hoofers*
Boston, Massachusetts

A tap company may be one answer, Europe another; but dancers and choreographers alike speak of the need for a strong personality, some charismatic dancer who can project the energy of tap in a creative way.

Tappers of yesterday and tomorrow: Fred Kelly (brother of Gene) with young students at his studio in New Jersey.

Before we relinquish custody of America's long-lost dance, let's be clear about what's needed, regardless of where it occurs.

> There's got to be somebody who comes along to be an inspiration, like Fred Astaire or Gene Kelly, to really bring it ahead. There's got to be one terrific personality, and he can change the course of music and dancing. So what you need is a tap messiah, somebody who'll come along and inspire everybody. These young guys coming along are studying like hell. One of them's going to jump out ahead of everybody else and be so terrific that people will look up to him. It won't be any guy who's young, although some guy in his twenties might come along; but as you look at any endeavor, whether it's ballet, tap, or anything else, it takes you fifteen years before you're great, for sure.
>
> —**George Church**
> tap and ballet dancer; appeared in
> the original casts of *On Your Toes*
> and *Oklahoma!*
> Naples, Florida

That's where tap stands in the mid-seventies. It's been revived, but not revitalized, not yet refashioned for our times. What's needed are expert tappers, innovative choreographers, and creative individuals with the conceptual and practical powers to put forth new musicals, new films, and new forms for the presentation of tap.

CHAPTER EIGHT

Do-It-Yourself—
Tap Patter Recovered

Tap is just about the hardest thing to explain. Just keep on tapping along.
That's about the size of it.
—John Bubbles
famous tap dancer; credited with
inventing the rhythm-tap style
Los Angeles, California

A little tapping is almost invariably dreadful.
—Paul Draper
in *Dance Magazine*, May, 1962

We've given you the history of tap dancing; tried to provide some sense
of how tap can evolve; and let you listen to dozens of amateur hoofers,
professional dancers, choreographers, and other people who have some
stake in tap dancing. We can do all that in a book, but we can't teach
you to tap dance. The complexities of the steps and their combinations, the
coordination of movement with music, the correction of mistakes—all of this
requires a fluidity of presentation that is beyond the capacity of the printed
page.

But we *can* help you to get started, or, if you are already a tapper, offer
some suggestions for improving your technique and some combinations for
you to try. In the following chapters, you can get some fine points and hints
on the proper approach to tap dancing. But if you really want to tap dance,
go out and take some lessons. Find a reputable tap instructor, preferably
one who has performing experience to validate his or her teaching
credentials.

Are you an amateur or a professional? You can avoid a great deal of
frustration and confusion by assessing your motivations for taking tap

dancing before you enroll in a class. If you have professional aspirations, then get serious. Find the best instructor in town, enroll in the most advanced class for which you qualify, and attend as often as is practical for you. Get the best equipment, practice diligently, and combine your tap skills with a wide range of singing, acting, and other dancing preparation.

If you plan to dance professionally, you'll find that elementary tap skills are no longer enough to boost your career. To make tap work for you in the theater or entertainment world, you'll need to demonstrate some degree of accomplishment. In addition, training in ballet and jazz dance styles will enhance your technical foundation.

> I'm sitting here now looking at one of Fred Astaire's tap shoes and one of Ginger Roger's tap shoes. I've got them in a glass case. Astaire says in a note on the top of the case: "To Pan, in memory of those thousands of rotten hours in rotten rehearsal halls."
>
> **—Hermes Pan**
> renowned film choreographer;
> staged dances for most of Astaire's
> films
> Beverly Hills, California

If, on the other hand, your interest in tap dancing is strictly at the amateur level, you can approach the activity from an altogether different perspective. Whether you want to pursue your own private star-fantasy, or dazzle and delight your friends, or find an entertaining way to have physical exercise, or relieve tension, or wear black patent leathers, or make funky noise with your feet—or all of the above—your ultimate aim is only to please yourself. And you will, of course. Did you ever see a tap dancer who wasn't smiling?

Dress so you can move comfortably, work up a sweat, and tap your troubles away. Above all, don't be ashamed of your amateur status.

> It's great to achieve amateur standing, that which is not necessarily professionally oriented. Relax, do it for yourself. Make that your objective.
>
> **—Murray Louis**

> All you have to do is listen to your instructor. Tell him that you're a beginner, and tell him not to lose his temper because you don't know your left foot from your right. Tell him, "As long as I get a kick out of it and I'm paying you, let me have my little world."
>
> **—Roye Dodge**
> well-known tap dance instructor
> and choreographer
> New City, New York

Don't worry about technical things such as timing or rhythmic analysis. You're not going to acquire a complete musical background in one hour a week. There are ways around it, too.

With me, I don't count. Never. I hear the music, whatever it may be, listen to it, and make up a routine to that certain music. I get the feeling of it and I *sing* my steps instead of counting them. Say, for instance, if a step goes: *be-dee-bop, be-dee-bop, be-dee-bop*, well, I do that with my feet. That's my type of counting. I never count because when you're thinking about the counting, you're thinking about how you're going to do the step, and when all this is running through your brain, it doesn't comprehend. I just feel the music, that's all, and it just comes out.

—Fayard Nicholas

However you deal with the beat, there's one tap matter you can't avoid: style. After all, that's why you're doing it, isn't it?

Create a style for yourself. Even an amateur can take tap dancing into an art form. Letting it happen naturally, of course, is the first thing. If you turn or come out of a turn and land a certain way, if that feels natural to you, then that's something in your brain telling you that that's your style.

—Jeff Parker
professional entertainer who tap
dances with Eleanor Powell in her
garage on Saturday mornings
Los Angeles, California

Equipment

You can tap dance in regular street shoes, but there's no adequate way to produce the right percussive sound without taps. If buying tap shoes is a financial problem, the next best thing is to attach metal taps to an old pair of leather-soled shoes.

Taps come in a variety of styles and sizes. Consider the various models and gauge the feel of each tap before purchasing a set. Be sure to fit the tap to your shoe so that the heel tap covers the entire heel and the toe tap covers the front of the sole from the ball of your foot forward.

If you are at all serious about tapping, however, you'll want to purchase a pair of genuine tap shoes. Today's fashions in women's tap shoes feature both low and two-inch heels, with plain leather straps or fancy ribbon ties. Men's tap shoes are a little pointy for today's trends. However, both sexes have a choice between soft kid leather and the notorious black patent shine that seems to be as much a part of tap dancing as the taps themselves.

Capezio's and Selva's are two of the biggest manufacturers of taps and tap shoes. For more information, contact them at:

Capezio's
1612 Broadway
New York, New York 10019
(212) 245-2130

Selva and Sons
1607 Broadway
New York, New York 10019
(212) 586-5140

This is important: When you take your taps to the shoemaker, chose screws instead of nails. Make sure the screws go straight in, so you won't cut up the dance floor; and see that the toe tap protrudes about an eighth of an inch beyond the tip of the shoe. Otherwise, when you make a toe sound, you will hear the dull thud of shoe leather and not the clear tap of metal. The top tap should be tight; but if the heel tap is slightly loose, it makes for a somewhat fuller sound. (Don't overdo it, however—heel taps should not be *too* loose.) Finally, have the shoemaker put thin rubber on the soles of your shoes. Not under the tap, of course, but from the back of the toe tap down along the sole. This will give you a firmer footing on the floor and keep you from slipping.

From the socks up, it's a matter of taste. Anything goes in tap class, from black leotards with silk racing stripes to hip-hugging jazz pants to baggy corduroys. Save the floor-length petticoats and the top hat and tails for that special performance, unless there's some special person in class you're really out to impress.

Music

Tap dancing makes its own music, that's true. You can tap to humming, whistling, or falling rain, but *real* music provides a rhythmic pattern that enhances the beauty of tap rhythms. You'll probably find that you prefer to tap to some kind of record or tape if you don't have your own live pianist.

It doesn't really matter what *kind* of music you tap to. You can purchase special tap dancing records at record stores and dance-supply outlets. These contain a variety of rhythmic settings that include challenging modern tempos, ethnic beats, and syncopated versions of tap classics such as "Tea for Two," "Once in Love with Amy," and "Pennies from Heaven."

If you're serious, you may want to pick up a secondhand variable-speed phonograph. These machines are invaluable for practicing in that they let you adjust the turntable speed to any pace desired. You can run through a routine slowly, then speed it up as you become more familiar with it.

Two very good tap albums are the Hoctor Dance Records "More Tunes for Tap" (DRLP 3061) and "Tap Happy" (DRLP 4013). These can be obtained, along with a complete catalog of tap albums, by writing to:

> Herbet Dancewear Company
> 902 Broadway
> New York, New York 10011

Practice

Whether you're amateur or professional, practice is absolutely essential. In a sense, your feet and body can be likened to a musical instrument, which requires a sustained investment of time in order to be played with skill. You simply can't go to class for an hour each week, let it go at that, and come away with much feeling for tap dancing. A certain amount of diligent practice is necessary. But chances are you'll love it. As with most pastimes, you'll find your enjoyment is directly proportional to the time you spend at it. Moreover, it's not until you've started tapping on your own, outside of dance class, that you begin to experience all the pleasure and excitement that comes from tap.

> I practice in the bathroom, where I have a tile floor. I try not to do it at particularly odd hours.
>
> **—Rob Hess**

Many tappers construct or purchase special tap mats. These portable dance surfaces roll up for easy storage and transport, insuring you of a hard tap surface wherever you want to tap. You can make your own tap mat out of thin strips of hardwood (oak or maple work well) cut about one inch wide and eight to ten feet long. Glue or rivet the strips to a piece of heavy canvas up to eighteen feet long. If that sounds like too much work, there are easier ways to come up with good tap surfaces.

> My whole family's going into it. We got ourselves a big sheet of Masonite, one-eighth-inch Masonite about four foot by twelve foot, and put it in our basement. Instead of tapping on the tile, where you'd nick it up, we tap on the Masonite. That's show biz.
>
> **—Jerry Teener**

Of course, the real fun begins once you take your tapping out of both the classroom and your home. On the street, in restaurants, supermarkets, other public places, tap dancing can transform an ordinary scene into your own movie set. It adds flair and raises spirit. Once you've overcome any self-consciousness, take pride in your tapping. Treat those around you to a taste of old-time hoofing.

> The place I practice is at work when I'm waiting for the elevators, on the marble floors. Everybody five floors either way knows exactly who it is. They either tell me to shut up or they applaud.
>
> **—Jack Gunther**
> amateur tapper
> New York, New York

Where you practice is your own business, as long as you observe local statutes.

> Back in the forties we used to meet on the corners and dance, but they had a late-hour law out in L.A. against disorderly conduct. We'd create a lot of excitement, and we'd all holler and laugh. So they picked us up and put most of us in jail. When we got ready to go before the judge, the judge asked me what was I doing and I said I was dancing. He said, "What kind of dancing?" and I told him. He said, "Let me see it," and I danced and he said, "You're a freak! Go on home," and I danced right on out of the courtroom.
>
> **—Sandman Sims**

Recitals and Other Hazards of the Trade

Once you've been tapping for a year or so, don't be surprised if your instructor starts preparing your class for a recital. Dance recitals vary according to the teacher and the studio. The main thing to remember is that you're not alone. In all likelihood, everyone there is as nervous, unsure, and in need of comforting as you.

> I have a recital every year in June. We work during the year on different routines, different types of numbers, not just for the adults but for everyone in general. I try to get a pretty balanced picture of dance, a couple of ballet numbers, some Hawaiian or Charleston, different novelty kinds of things to make it an exciting revue. We do approximately forty-two numbers in two hours, involving about three hundred people. My recital is the highlight of the year. We give four performances and we're usually sold out maybe two weeks in advance. I suppose we go through the usual types of accidents. Somebody will wet themselves maybe once a year—one of the kids, that is.
>
> —**Dawn Crafton**
> tap instructor
> Rockville, Maryland

For those who worry about hurting themselves there is good news and bad news. The good news is that tap injuries are extremely rare. The bad news is that they can be terribly damaging.

> In *Oklahoma!* I kicked a couple of people on stage. I played Will Parker and I put them in the hospital. Once you kick somebody with your taps, it's a very rough thing.
>
> —**Michael Dominico**
> tap dancer, instructor, and
> choreographer; the only tapper
> today performing Morton Gould's
> *Tap Dance Concerto*
> New York, New York

Now, before you chicken out, get hold of some taps, get hold of some music, and get hold of yourself. Remember, dancing is its own reward, but *tap* makes you happy.

CHAPTER NINE

Jerry Ames on Tap

There is a quotation in this book in which a writer and critic expresses alarm at a young dancer's ambition to pursue a career as a tap dancer. His reaction suggests that such a goal is, for all practical purposes, illusory, perhaps laughable.

Tap, in spite of a reprise brought about by nostalgia, is supposed to be long dead. Why, then, does the mummy continue to excite audiences young and old when it is unwrapped for presentation? Why, indeed, should not an aspirant feel hopeful enough to believe that in a healthy, thriving dance world there can be yet another alternative to joining one of the many ballet, modern, Spanish, or other ethnic dance companies that abound? Why should the writer have found that youngster's goal almost ludicrous?

In the lean years of the fifties and sixties, there were tap performers, black and white, who gave their lives to perfecting their art, clinging to it in the face of every frustration, sometimes taking the most demeaning jobs out of economic necessity, but never ceasing to practice, to hold on to the steps, the technique that could wither with neglect. More than dedication, it was love—for some, with the attrition of the years, a desperate, futile love.

The patronizing, cavalier attitude toward tap dancing and tap dancers does us all a disservice. Given the opportunity, tap could lend itself very effectively and uniquely to the expression of contemporary choreographic themes, whether in the musical theater, films, or on television. Like ballet, jazz, or modern dance, tap is only as limited as the talent and imagination of the choreographer. What the dance director must have—and this is crucial—are dedicated dancers equipped with the necessary training to execute the choreography.

To laud tap in this way is not to disparage other great dance forms. Variety, after all, fights boredom and brings diversity to entertainment. It is worth noting that when *Gunsmoke* became a highly rated success on television, the rival channels were quickly saturated with pale imitations until prime time was virtually lassoed. The same was true with the medical series; we were soon subjected to a spate of similar shows including *Dr. Kildare, The Doctors, The Nurses, Medical Center, The Interns, Ben Casey,* ad nauseum. Where was the daring to be different?

This is not a plea for the restoration of tap as the primary form of dance on the Broadway stage or in any other medium. It is simply hoped that choreographers will seek to broaden the means of expression at their disposal. A particular type of music or mood in a production might lend itself best to ballet sequence, another scene possibly to jazz or modern dance, and yet another to a rousing tap specialty. It certainly depends, in more ways than one, upon the talent at hand. If young dancers are adequately trained in *all* the various dance forms, the alternatives available to choreographers, not to mention the dance world in general, will be that much richer.

The Jerry Ames Tap Company. *Left to right* Cinda Mast, Gary McKay, Kathy Burke, Jerry Ames, Diana Moore, David Finch, and Jenny Rizzo. *Jack Mitchell.*

Kathy Burke and Gary McKay in "Waltz Time," from The Jerry Ames Tap Dance Company.
Jack Mitchell.

Perhaps the most disturbing attitude to the professional tap dancer today is that which views tap as a relatively simple dance form of limited vocabulary, consisting principally of time steps, Shuffle Off to Buffaloes, Maxie Fords, and other cliché steps of the past. Nothing could be further from the truth. The innovation is there for those who choose to recognize it.

Now, I am speaking here of the survival and growth of tap as a performing art and the need for qualified talent. This argument does not pertain to the ebullient army of office workers and housewives around the country who have discovered that taking tap dancing once or twice a week with their local dancing teacher is a fun way to exercise. I certainly don't mean to put down their enthusiasm, and I'm more than happy that they have

131

discovered the joys of tap. Being a teacher as well as a performer, I welcome and encourage new tappers, no matter what their degree of competence. But there is a need for young, dedicated, aspiring, professional dancers to strive for the ultimate in tap technique, supported by a solid foundation in ballet and jazz dancing.

It saddened me when, after seeing the magnificent tap dance of Fred Astaire and Eleanor Powell to "Begin the Beguine" in the film *That's Entertainment (I),* I overheard a young couple say, "It's a shame tap is an art that will die with Fred Astaire and Eleanor Powell." Why? Ballet did not die with Nijinski. With encouragement, enthusiasm, and hope for a rewarding career, can we not produce future Astaires, Powells, Robinsons, Kellys, and Millers?

In 1975, having concluded that one small way to help sustain the interest in this dance form was to establish a tap company, I founded the Jerry Ames Tap Dance Company. I hope it will be a forerunner of other companies to come. Our goal is to preserve the great traditional dances and at the same time encourage new and innovative works using the tap idiom.

In time, hopefully, we will cease to belabor the issue of whether tap is dead or alive. Given the continuing opportunity for life, there should no longer be any question of tap's survival. Treated as any other respected member in the family of American dance, tap will endure, growing healthily and possibly making some surprising new contributions uniquely its own.

Instruction

CHAPTER TEN

Tap Technique:

If you've never taken a tap lesson, you will learn something from reading this chapter—tap terminology, the basic foot movements, a few simple steps perhaps, and, if you are very clever, a rudimentary routine. But this book, as we have stated, will not really teach you to tap dance. For that you need a teacher—to demonstrate the steps, to show you the fluidity of body movement, to help you correct mistakes, to encourage you. Nonetheless, the pages that follow will give you a feel for the technique of tap and something of what it's like to take a lesson.

If you are a student of tap, no matter what your level of skill, there is something here that will be helpful to you. It may be the practice exercises, it may be the advanced routines. If you can take what you already know and apply it in these exercises, you are bound to benefit.

Beginning Tap Technique

The first thing a neophyte tap dancer must learn when approaching a tap step is to separate the ball of the foot from the heel. Thus, the initial movement I teach is simply to walk in rhythm around the room, lifting the legs in a strutlike movement, landing on the ball of the foot as the arms swing in natural opposition to the feet. (Often, for the self-conscious beginner, the natural seems surprisingly difficult, so that when I say, "Simply walk and swing your arms the way you usually do," suddenly the left arm shoots out with the left foot and vice versa.)

One must also learn at the outset to coordinate the arms with the leg movement. From the start, I stress control of the arms. If you concentrate solely on footwork, neglecting the rest of your body, although you will learn to move your feet nimbly as you execute tap sounds, as time passes you will have no control from the waist up. Before getting into any bad habits, which are most difficult to unlearn, take the approach that you aspire to dance with your whole body—arms, feet, head, etc. Then, as you get into more difficult footwork, the rest of your body will dance with placement and control.

Vocabulary of Basic Tap Terms

Before we start discussing actual steps, however, it is important that you understand the language of tap. The glossary that follows will make comprehensible what might otherwise seem cryptic.

Tap (or Touch): single tap sound made by touching the ball of the foot to the floor, then lifting it, keeping the weight on the other foot.

Step (or Ball): single tap sound made by stepping on the ball of the foot; can be made in place or stepping out—forward, back, or side.

Heel (or Heel drop): single tap sound made by raising the heel off the floor, keeping the ball of the foot on the floor, then placing the heel down.

Step–heel: two tap sounds made by raising the foot off the floor, stepping on the ball, and then dropping the heel.

Brush: single tap sound made by touching the front tap on the floor as the foot swings forward. At the end of the brush, the foot remains off the floor.

Shuffle: two tap sounds made by brushing forward and then brushing back (front shuffle), or brushing out and then brushing in (side shuffle). At the end of the shuffle, the foot remains off the floor.

Toe: single tap sound made by raising the foot and touching the front edge of the toe tap, which should protrude slightly from the tip of the shoe, to the floor.

Hop: single tap sound made by hopping on the ball of one foot.

Jump: single tap sound made by jumping from one foot and landing on the ball of the other foot.

Stamp: single tap sound made by placing the whole foot firmly on the floor.

Spank: single tap sound made by hitting the ball of the front tap on the

Cramp Roll:
Right ball of foot,
left ball of foot.

Cramp Roll:
Right heel,
left heel
reverse.

Lunge: Lunge on left foot with bent knee. Left knee straight pointing toe (turned out).

David Finch and Diana Moore, members of The Jerry Ames Tap Dance Company, are pictured in the demonstrations.
Photographs by Scott Star.

floor as you bring the foot back. At the end of the spank, the foot remains off the floor.

Scuff: single tap sound made by raising the foot and hitting the heel tap on the floor as the foot moves forward.

Drag: sliding tap sound made by stepping back on one foot and sliding the other foot back on the floor.

Chug: sliding tap sound made by starting on the ball of the foot and sliding forward as the heel drops down.

Flap (or Slap): two tap sounds made by brushing the foot forward and then stepping on the ball of the same foot.

Flap-heel: three tap sounds made by adding a heel drop to a flap on the same foot.

138

Flaps: Flap right, flap left with arms extended in opposition to the feet.

139

Brush: (The right foot has just tapped the floor with the front tap as the foot was lifted forward.)

Hop Shuffles: Hopping on the ball of the left foot, followed by a shuffle on the right foot. Try eight hop shuffles, then reverse, hopping on the right foot.

Ball change: two tap sounds made by changing from the ball of one foot to the ball of the other.

Shuffle–ball change: four tap sounds made by shuffling one foot, stepping on the ball of the same foot, then changing to the ball of the other foot.

Cramp roll: four tap sounds made by stepping on the ball of one foot, then the ball of the other, then the heel of the first foot, followed by the heel of the second. Cramp rolls can be done in place or traveling to either side. The first foot always steps in the direction of movement.

Toe: Tapping the tip of the toe.

Lunge: single tap sound made by stepping, with a bent knee, to front or side, shifting the weight onto the lunging foot.

Pullback (or Pickup): advanced tap sound made by spanking on one foot with the other foot off the floor, then landing on the ball of the same foot.

Double pullback: four tap sounds made by starting on the balls of both feet, pullback one, then pullback the other, landing in the same order.

Nerve tap: rapid tapping of one foot on the floor, keeping the weight on the other foot.

Wing: three tap sounds made on one foot by scraping the side of the foot outward from the body, brushing in, then stepping on the ball of the foot. Throughout the movement, the other foot remains off the floor.

Double wing: a wing done with both feet at the same time.

Basic Tap Steps

Let's begin with a basic step. Step out on the ball of the right foot and drop the right heel. Then reverse—left ball, left heel—arms reaching in opposition. Now for some simple combinations. Count out the steps as indicated beneath each instruction.

1. Step–heel Combination

Step R, Heel R, Step L, Heel L

1   &   2   &

Now, twice as fast, in place:

Step R, Heel R, Step L, Heel L,

1   &   2   &

Step R, Heel R, Step L, Heel L.

3   &   4   &

2. Toe–heel Combination

A toe sound is made by hitting the front edge of the shoe on the floor with the heel upraised. Try this simple toe combination.

Step R, Heel R, Step L, Heel L,

1   &   2   &

Step R, Heel R, Step L, Heel L,

3   &   4   &

143

> Step R, Heel R, Toe L (cross in back of R), Heel R,
>
> 5   &   6   &
>
> Step L, Heel L, Toe R (cross in back of L), Heel L.
>
> 7   &   8   &

In this exercise, keep your left arm extended in front with the right arm in back throughout.

3. Flap–heel Combination

Remember, a flap, sometimes called a slap, consists of two sounds: sliding or brushing out on the ball of the foot, then stepping on the ball of the same foot. Now, for a combination, try eight flaps (remember, on the ball), alternating right and left. Then try eight flap–heels, again alternating. To execute the flap–heel, complete the flap and then drop the heel of the same foot, producing three distinct sounds. Keep practicing, start slowly and then speed up. Eight flaps, eight flap–heels. After it comes without difficulty, try it sideways. First move to the right: eight side flaps, eight side flap–heels. Then alternate to the left side. After you've mastered that, try it backwards. Do eight backflaps (brushing backward), eight backflap–heels.

Now you have a useful exercise for developing sharp flaps and flap–heels. Once you can do it in all directions, try doing it in a square pattern, first going forward, then side R, then back, then side L.

4. Shuffle Combinations

A shuffle consists of two sounds. Standing on the left foot, brush the right foot forward on the front tap. Then brush it back, lifting it off the floor. Front, back. Front, back. Do it on the right foot eight times and then switch to the left. Shuf-fle, shuf-fle, shuf-fle, etc.

A double shuffle is two quick shuffles on the same foot. Now try this combination:

> Shuffle R (front), Shuffle R (to the side)
> Shuffle R (front), Shuffle R (side)
>
> Then: Double shuffle (front), double shuffle (side).

In other words: Shuffle R

> front, side, front, side,
> front, front, side, side.

Now try it on the left foot.

To clear up some possible confusion between a shuffle and a flap, they

Flap Heel: Flap the ball of the
right foot.

Flap Heel: Place right heel down. (Notice weight over right foot with knee slightly bent.)

both consist of two sounds, but a flap stays on the floor and a shuffle lifts off. Here is one last shuffle exercise:

Shuffle R, Step R (on the ball), Shuffle L, Step L,
  & a   1   & a   2

Shuffle R, Step R, Shuffle L, Step L.
  & a   3   & a   4

Shuffle R, Step R, Heel R, Shuffle L, Step L, Heel L,
  & 1   &   2   & 3   &   4

Shuffle R, Step R, Heel R, Shuffle L, Step L, Heel L.
  & 5   &   6   & 7   &   8

That is four shuffle steps followed by four shuffle step–heels.

5. Shuffle–ball change Combination

A ball change consists of changing from the ball of one foot to the ball of the other. I shall sometimes use the abbreviation B.C. for ball change:

Shuffle R, B.C. (R ball, L ball)

Now try this combination:

Flap R, Heel R, Flap L, Heel L,
  a 1 &   a 2 &

Flap R, Heel R, Shuffle L, B.C. (L ball to R ball).
  a 3 &   a 4 &

Now reverse, L side (Flap L, Heel L, etc.). Do this three times, alternating R, L, R, then go into the break:

Flap L, Heel L, Shuffle R, B.C.
  a 1   2   & 3   & 4

Flap R, Heel R, Shuffle L, B.C.
  a 5   6   & 7   & 8

Begin the combination again, starting on the left foot.

Walking Six Tap Riff : Right toe.

Walking Six Tap Riff: Scuff
right heel forward.

Walking Six Tap Riff: Drop left heel.

Walking Six Tap Riff: Bring heel down, hitting back tip of tap.

Walking Six Tap Riff: Put down front tap of right foot.

Walking Six Tap Riff : Put down heel of right foot. Alternate entire step beginning on left foot.

6. Hop–shuffle Combination

Hop on the ball of the left foot, then Shuffle R.

Now try this combination:

> Hop L Shuffle R, Hop L Shuffle R,
>
>   1   & a   2   & a

> Hop L Shuffle R, Hop L.
>
>   3   & a   4

Now reverse:

> Hop R Shuffle L, Hop R Shuffle L,
>
>   5   &a   6   & a

> Hop R Shuffle L, Hop R.
>
>   7   & a   8

That is three hop–shuffles and then a hop on each side. After doing the count of four on each side, do seven hop–shuffles (Hop L Shuffle R) and then a final Hop L. Reverse the whole step, Hopping R, Shuffling L.

7. Stamp–ball Change Combination

A stamp is made by putting the whole foot on the floor. Let's try a step containing stamps, shuffles, and ball changes:

> Stamp R (cross in front of L), B.C. (L to R),
>
>   1   2 3

> Stamp L (cross in front of R), B.C. (R to L),
>
>   4   5 6

> Shuffle R, B.C. (R to L).
>
> & 7   & 8

Now reverse, Stamp L, etc.

Do this three times, starting with Stamp R, then go into the break:

Step R, Shuffle L, B.C. (L to R),

  1   & 2 & 3

Step L, Shuffle R, B.C. (R to L),

  4   & 5 & 6

Stamp R (cross in front of L) (hold).

  7   8

Now repeat, reversing the whole combination, starting with

Stamp L (cross in front of R), etc.

Intermediate Combinations

8. Double Time Step

Stamp R (in front) Hop L Shuffle R, Step R (in back),

  8   1   & a   2

Flap L (in front), Step R (in back), Stamp L (in front).

& 3   &   4

Now reverse:

Hop R Shuffle L, Step L,

  5   & a   6

Flap R, Step L (Stamp R—same as 8 above).

& 7   &   (8)

Repeat three times, then do the break:

Hop L (in back) Shuffle R (side),

  1   & a

Step R, Shuffle L (side),

  2   & 3

155

Double Time Step: Shuffle right, step right (on ball, in back).

Spank R, Heel L, Step R (in back),
           &   a   1

Spank L, Heel R, Step L (in back),
           &   a   2

Spank R, Heel L, Step R,
           &   a   3

Spank L, Heel R, Step L,
           &   a   4

Double Time Step: Hop on the ball of the left foot.

Step L, Shuffle R (front),

&   4 &

Hop L, Flap R (in front),
5   & 6

Step L (in back), Stamp R (in front), (hold).
&   7   8

9. Spank–heel–step Combination (traveling backwards)

Double Time Step: Stamp right foot in front (keeping weight on the back foot).

Spank R, Heel L, Step R,
        &   a   5

Heel R, Heel L, Spank L,
        &   a   6

Heel R, Step L (in back), Heel L,
        &   a   7

Heel R, Heel L, Scuff R.
        &   a   8

Repeat this combination three times, then go into the break:

Double Time Step: Flap left forward, step right (ball) in back.

Double Time Step: Stamp left foot in front. (Repeat from #1 alternating left side, right side, six times.)

Spank R, Heel L, Step R (in back),

   &   a   1

Heel R, Heel L, Spank L,

   &   a   2

Heel R, Step L (in back), Heel L,

   &   a   3

Heel R, Heel L, Scuff R.

   &   a   4

Repeat break.

10. Hop–shuffle–hop–step–heel–toe Combination (traveling right)

Hop R Shuffle L, Hop R Shuffle L, Hop R,

  1   & 2   &   3   &   4

Step–heel L (cross in front), Toe R (in back),

  &   5   6

Step R, Step L (cross in front).

  7   8

Repeat three times, then go into the break:

Cramp roll R (starting on the ball of the right foot),

  1 & a 2

Cramp roll R, Cramp roll R

  3 & a 4   5 & a 6

Heel R Heel L, Heel R Heel L.

  &   7   &   8

Now repeat the entire combination, reversing (Hop L Shuffle R) and moving to the left.

Shuffle Off to Buffalo: Stamp right foot. Then shuffle the left foot.

Shuffle Off to Buffalo: Hop to left foot as you bend knee of right foot, bending arms at the same time. Repeat from step #1 moving sideways.

Intermediate/Advanced Tap Routines

Step Lively!

Music: "Sweet Georgia Brown"
Hoctor Dance Record #H-704A

Step 1

Flap–Heel R, Step–Heel L (X front), Cramp Roll, Touch R to Side,
  1 &   2 &   3 &   4

Heel Drop L, Double Shuffle R (repeat), Step R (back), Drag L,
  &   5 & 6 &   7

Step L, X Step R (front), Chug L, Drop Heel L (lunge position),
  & 8   &

2 L Heel Drops, Hop L, Heel Drop L (turning R), Heel L, Heel L,
  1 2   3   4   5   6

Step R (X front), Heel R, Step L, Drag R, BC (turning R), Stamp R,
  7   8   1   2   &3   4

Flap L, Brush R, Stamp R, Flap L, Brush R, Stamp RL.   (8 Meas.)
  & 5   &   6   & 7   &   a8

Step 2

(traveling back) Spank R, Heel L, Step R, Spank L, Heel R, Step L,
                 &   1   &   2   &   3

Spank R, Heel L, Step R, Spank L, Heel R (X front), Step L, Spank R,
  &   4   &   5   &   6   &

Heel L, Step R, Spank L, Heel R, Step L, Spank R, Heel L, (X front),
  7   &   8   &   1   &   2

Step R, Spank L, Heel R, Step L, Spank–Heel–Step, (4 times RLRL),

    &   3   &   4   & a 5 & a 6 & a 7 & a 8

Repeat Step 2, but Stamp L instead of Step L.   (8 meas.)

Step 3

Flap R, Brush L, Stamp L, (repeat 3 times), Flap R, Brush L, Step L,

  & 1   &   2   & 7   &   a
  & 3   &   4
  & 5   &   6

Stamp R (reverse entire Step on L side), Scuff R (X front), Hop L,

8   1   2

Flap R, Shuffle L, B.C., Flap L, Brush R, B.C. (turning L), Step R (X front),

 & 3 & 4   &5 & 6   & 7   &8   1

Step L, Drag R, B.C., Step R, Chug Heel Drop R, Chug Heel Drop L.

 2   3   &4   5   6   7   HOLD 8

                            (8 Meas.)

Step 4

Step R, Drag L, Drop Heel R (reverse), Step R, Heel R, Heel L, Flap R,

 1   &   2   5   &   6   & 7
 3   &   4

(into L foot), Heel L, Heel R, Repeat Step 4, Starting Step L (½ turn R)

              &   8

Step L, Brush R, B.C., Step R, Brush L, B.C., Chug Heel L, Chug Heel L,

 1   & 2 &3   4   & 5   &6   7   8

Chainé, Chainé, R (2 turns to RO, Step R, Heel Drop R, Heel Drop R.

 1 2   3 4   5   6   7   HOLD 8

                         (8 Meas.)

Step 5

Flap L, Heel R, Heel L, Spank R, Heel L, Shuffle R, Heel L, Shuffle R,

  1   &   2   &   3 & a   4   & a

Heel L Shuffle R, Cramp Roll R, Heel R, Heel L (reverse starting R side),

  5   & a 6 & a 7   &   8

Flap L, Shuffle R, Heel L (turning L), 4 Shuffles R and L Heel Drops (4),

& 1 & a   2   & a 3
                         & a 4
                         & a 5
                         & a 6

Shuffle R, Cramp Roll R, Repeat to R from Flap R4 shuffles (turning R).

& a   7 & a 8   (8 Meas.)

Step 6

Repeat first 4 bars of Step 5, Step R, Drag L, B.C. (½ turn R), Step L,

                              1   & 2 &3

Drag R, B.C. (completing turn), 2 Heel Drops R (in lunge).

& 5   &6   7 8

Reverse entire step from Step R or 5th bar of music

Step 7

Repeat Step 1.

Step 8

Repeat first 4 bars of Step 2, Spank R, Heel L, Step R, Spank L, Heel R,

                            &   1   &   2   &

Step L, Spank R, Heel L, Step R, Spank L, Heel R, Step L (X front),

  3   &   4   &   5   &   6

Step R, Stamp L (in lunge), 3 Spot Turns R, Jump Lunge R.

                                            (8 Meas.)

Easy Does It

Music: "Love Is a Simple Thing"
Hoctor Dance Record #H-7-2714B

Step 1

Hop L, Flap R, Flap L, Flap R, Flap L, Shuffle R (front) Shuffle R (side),
    &   a-1 &2   &3   &4   &5   &a

Step R, Step L, Heel LXF, Brush R, Step Heel R, Brush L (Bk Arabesque),
  6   &   a   7   & 8   1   Hold 2

Step L, Step RXF, Step L into pique turn L, Step R, Step L, Flap–Heel &
   &   3   4   5   &   6   &7   &

Brush L.
  8

Step 2

*Step L bk, Step R bk, Step L fwd, Step R fwd, Brush L fwd, Hop R,
      1   &   2   &   3   &

Heel drop R, Step L, Shuffle R, B.C. (turning R), Flap R, Shuffle L
      4   &   5& a 6   &a   7   &

B.C. (X front).
 a 8

*Repeat from Step L bk   (8 Meas.)

Step 3

Slide R, Step L, Step RXFL—REPEAT
   1 &   2   3&4

Step L, Shuffle R, B.C. (turning L), Flap R, Shuffle L, B.C. (X front).
   &   5&   a 6   &a7&   a 8

Repeat from Step 3 Slide R (back to audience).

Step 4

*Flap L, Shuffle R, B.C., Flap R, Shuffle L, B.C., Flap L, Shuffle R,
   &a   1& a 2   &a   3& a 4   &a   5&

B.C., Shuffle R, B.C., B.C.
a 6   &a 7& a 8

Flap L, Shuffle R, B.C., Flap R, Shuffle L, B.C., Flap L, Shuffle R,
   &a   1& a 2   &a   3& a 4   &a   5&

B.C., B.C., B.C., B.C. (turning L).
a 6 & a 7 & a 8

Step 5

*Hop L, Brush R, Scuff R, Heel L, Slide Bk L (landing R), Jump L,
   a   &   a   1   &   2   &

Shuffle R, Hop L, Step RXBL, Toe LXFR, Hop R, Step LXFR, Toe RXFL,
  3& a   4   & a   5   &

Hop L, Step LXBR, Toe L, Hop R, B.C., B.C.
  a   6   &   a   7 & a 8
*Repeat from Step 5

Step 6

*Hop L, Brush R, Scuff R (sideways), Heel L, Step R, Step LXFR, Hop L,
   a   &   a   1   &   2   &

Brush R, Scuff R (sideways), Heel L, Step R, Step LXFR, Flap–heel R,
  a   3   &   4   &a   5

Toe L (turn R Pique), B.C., B.C., *REPEAT from Step 6.
   &   a6&a 7 & a 8   (8 Meas.)

Step 7

*(In profile Left) Hop L, Shuffle R, Hop L (Point R touch front)

&	1&	a	2	
"	" "	"	"	back)
&	3&	a	4	

Brush R, Hop L, Step R, Brush L, Hop R, Step L (profile Right),

& 5	& 6	& 7

Jump R (point touch back) L

&	8

*Repeat from Step R—Alternate Side through count 7—Step L, Step R.

&	8

Step 8

*Step L, Step R, Flap Bk L, Step R, Brush L, Hop R, Step L, B.C.,

&	1	&a	2	&	a	3 & 4

2 Waltz Clogs starting Flap R
&a5&a6 &a7&a8

*Repeat from Step 8. Brush Back R, Hop L, Brush Front R, Hop L,.

&	1	&	2

Brush RXL, Hop L, Step R, Step L, 2 Waltz Clogs (traveling fwd)

&	3	&	4	&a5&a6 &a7&a8

Brush R, Hop L, Step R, Brush L, Hop R, Step L, Brush R, Hop L

&	a	1	&	a	2	&	a

Step R, Brush L, Hop R, Step L, Step R, Step L, Brush R Front,

3	&	a	4	&	5	&

Brush RXB, Toe RXF—Flip R Hand same time as Toe R.   (12 Meas.)

6	7

Bibliography

Books

Atwater, Constance, **Tap Dancing.** Rutland, Vt., C. E. Tuttle, 1971.

Duggan, Anne Schley, **Tap Dances.** New York, A. S. Barnes & Co., 1932.

Ewen, David, **The Story of America's Musical Theater.** Philadelphia, Chilton Book Company, 1961, rev. ed. 1968.

Frost, Helen, **Tap, Caper and Clog.** New York, A. S. Barnes & Co., 1931.

Hungerford, Mary Jane, **Creative Tap Dancing.** New York, Prentice-Hall, 1939.

Nash, Barbara, **Tap Dance.** Dubuque, Ia., W. C. Brown Company Publishers, 1969.

O'Gara, Shiela, **Tap It.** New York, A. S. Barnes & Co., 1937.

Sauthoff, Hermine, **Tap Dance for Fun.** New York, A. S. Barnes & Co., 1931.

Shomer, Louis, **Tip Top Tapping.** New York, Louellen, 1937.

Stearns, Marshall and Stearns, Jean, **Jazz Dance.** New York, The Macmillan Company, 1968.

Thompson, Howard, **Fred Astaire, A Pictorial Treasury of His Films.** New York, Falcon Enterprises, 1970.

Vallance, Tom, **The American Musical.** New York, Castle Books, 1970.

Wade, Rosalind, **Tap Dancing in 12 Easy Lessons.** Philadelphia, David McKay Company, 1936.

Periodicals

"Astaire to Run Tap Schools," **Dance News** (December, 1946).

Draper, Paul, numerous articles in **Dance Magazine** (from August, 1954, through September, 1963, including: 8/54, 1/57, 7/57, 2/62, 5/62, 6/62, 8/62, 9/62, 11/62, 3/63, 8/63, 9/63).

Horosko, Marian, "Tap, Tapping and Tappers," **Dance Magazine** (October, 1971).

Knight, Arthur, "Dancing in Films," **Dance Index** (August, 1947).

Jay, Leticia, "The Wonderful Old-time Hoofers at Newport," **Dance Magazine** (August, 1963).

Manning, Betty, "Tap Marches On," **Dance Magazine** (October, 1944).

Terry, Walter, "Tap Dance Trend," New York **Herald Tribune** (August 31, 1941).

Todd, Arthur, "From Chaplin to Kelly: The Dance on Film," **Theatre Arts** (August, 1951).

Films

The History of Jazz Dancing, 1970. 56 min. Lecture demonstration by Les Williams presenting the black man's role in the history of jazz dancing. New York Public Library, The Performing Arts Research Center, Lincoln Center.

Uncle Tom's Cabin, 1903. 21 min. Drama of the original novel, produced by Thomas A. Edison, shows early examples of time step, breaks, the strut, and Cakewalk. New York Public Library, The Performing Arts Research Center, Lincoln Center.

Index

INDEX